Whose Offering
Plate Is It?

More praise for *Whose Offering Plate Is It?*

"Clif Christopher has done it again. For years his love for Christ, love for the church, and his practical wisdom about stewardship, fund-raising, and capital campaigns have inspired and taught me. Now he has collected many of the tough questions lay and clergy leaders ask about financing church ministry and provided his best insights. This is a book worth owning and reading!"

Scott J. Jones, Bishop, Kansas Area of
The United Methodist Church and
author of *The Evangelistic Love of God and Neighbor*

"A wake-up call for every church leader seeking to maximize mission contributions in a downsized economy. Clif reminds us of the intense competition for the nonprofit dollar. People contribute to mission that has significance and demonstrates measurable results. They do not give to ill-defined, self-serving church budgets. A timely read!"

Mike Slaughter, author of *Change the World*

"Clif's book is truly a gift to pastors, a great gift that will help all pastors do a better job every day. I am chairman of the board of a seminary, and I will recommend that we provide each student with Clif's book as a tool kit to help them for many, many years."

Jerre Stead, Chairman and CEO of IHS, Inc.

Whose Offering Plate Is It?

J. Clif Christopher

Abingdon Press
Nashville

WHOSE OFFERING PLATE IS IT?

Copyright © 2010 by Abingdon Press

This book is printed on acid-free paper.

Library of Congress Cataloging-in-Publication Data

Christopher, J. Clif.
  Whose offering plate is it? / J. Clif Christopher.
    p. cm.
  ISBN 978-1-4267-1013-1 (book - pbk./trade pbk. : alk. paper) 1. Church fund raising. I. Title.
  BV772.5.C47 2010
  254'.8—dc22

                                                              2010027221

10 11 12 13 14 15 16 17 18 19—10 9 8 7 6 5 4 3 2 1

MANUFACTURED IN THE UNITED STATES OF AMERICA

Contents

Introduction

In 2008 I wrote a little book called *Not Your Parents' Offering Plate*. In that book I argued for a complete change of culture in the way most mainline churches are doing stewardship. It was painfully obvious to me as I worked around the country that most church leaders did not get it and certainly had no idea why giving to religion as a whole was down nearly 50 percent from where it used to be. The evidence showed that America was not choosing the church for its charitable gifts the way it once had, yet most churches were still continuing to make the same old appeals in the same old way.

The title of the last book came from the old Oldsmobile commercial that used the phrase "Not your Father's Oldsmobile" in an attempt to encourage younger people to invest in their cars. The slogan was introduced about twelve years before the company declared that the Oldsmobile brand would be phased out.

Recently I have been painfully reminded of the dangers of offering slogans instead of real change. General Motors, the parent company of Oldsmobile, used to sell more than 50 percent of all the automobiles in America. It was an iconic brand—at one time the strongest company in America. GM took the brand for granted and assumed that people's loyalty would never waver no matter what. They put a dealership in every small town in America and paid outrageous sums to their labor force while guaranteeing them a lifetime of ease in retirement. *No problem, GM thought, we may have to raise prices a bit and cut a corner or two on quality, but Americans will still come running to us when they want a vehicle.*

Over a couple of decades, GM's market share began to drop. No significant changes were made. They tried some new slogans but did not make many new cars that were smaller and more fuel efficient. People began to notice that they were in the repair shop a lot. Some new guys showed up on the scene from Japan, and storm clouds began to brew. Yet GM still just continued the same basic package using the same model that had gotten them to number one years before.

We all know the outcome. Today, this iconic brand that used to sell 50 percent of all the cars in America sells less than 20 percent. If it were not for the U.S. government, there might not be a General Motors today.

To me the parallels with the church are frightening. Fifty-five percent of all charitable dollars used to go to the church. Today it is 33 percent. Sixty percent of America used to go to worship on Sunday mornings, and today it is closer to 40 percent. In some western states church attendance is closer to 20 percent. Can we not see the handwriting on the wall? Do we not realize that the "same old same old" is failing?

I do not argue for a new slogan. I argue for real change based on an understanding that if we are to reach the donor in 2011 then we have to speak in a language he or she understands and be prepared to defend the cause to which we are asking people to contribute. We must raise the bar of expectations and not make church "easier" than in days past. We must communicate effectively in ways that today's donors understand and not just pass an offering plate. We must learn accountability so people will see how their money is being used, not just go around trying to "out guilt" other causes. We have to realize that 1.8 million nonprofit organizations would be delighted to accept the same dollars that we want, and some of them might even argue that God is more on their side than ours.

In short, the previous book argued for the church to learn to compete, which is a dirty word to many in the church business. Just going on the assumption that people will support us because we are the church no longer cuts it.

Once the book came out and people read about the radical change in thinking that I was advocating, I received numerous questions about just how pastors and lay leaders should think and act in this new culture. Many of these were procedural questions about how to implement what they were coming to believe in. Thus this book was created to deal directly and simply with those questions. Each chapter is centered on a question I have received.

One of the first questions I received came from a young pastor in north Texas. Near the end of one of my speeches on the changes needed he raised his hand and asked, "Do you really believe this or is this just your gimmick?" What an intriguing question. He had obviously attended gatherings where the speaker passionately advocated for one thing but frankly did not follow his own teachings. It was just his canned speech. You need to know that my passion for change in Christian financial stewardship is not just my gig. It is truly my passion. I am firmly convinced that the only institution on the face of the planet that can possibly change the world is the church. No army, no government, and no nonprofit has the power to change the hearts of people like the body of Jesus Christ, and as those hearts change then so does practice, and so does the world. Effective financial stewardship helps the church get its funding to facilitate that change. Thus I am passionate about the church doing such stewardship as effectively and efficiently as we can— not to raise more money but to change the world.

My grandmother had a beautiful painted plate that hung in her den. It had been there for as long as I could remember. As a boy I used to run around in her home paying little attention to what I was doing or where I was going. My running path took me right in front of her painted plate. No one ever said to me, "Don't hurt the couch," or "Don't hit that mirror," but on almost a daily basis while visiting, one of my parents would say, "Be careful with the plate," or "Don't hurt that plate." I never quite understood why some old plate was so important. I frankly thought more about my running and dodging skills than that old plate. After all, it had always been there and always would be. No big deal. Then one day, it happened. As I turned the corner, paying attention to something else, I brushed the plate and down it came. To this day I can see it almost as if in slow motion, falling to the tile floor and shattering into a hundred pieces. I just froze. My grandmother was in the room when it happened, and the look on her face was one of absolute, profound sadness. She was not angry. She was hurt. I had callously broken my beloved grandmother's heart. She saw my frozen expression and came over to me after gently picking up all the pieces and placing them in a sack. She said, "This plate came from Germany. It was a gift from your father after the war ended. More than any other remembrance, this plate reminds me of the hardships and suffering that we all endured during that time in our lives. It was not easy for your father to bring back such a plate. He could hardly afford it at the time and just protecting it in a duffle bag as he flew home took great effort. It has always reminded me of his love for me and my love for him."

I had no idea. And I am not sure that I would have understood if someone had told me earlier. But when I saw the pain on my grandmother's face, heard the sadness and loss in her voice, and saw the tear creep from her eye, I knew that I had trifled with something precious. It was not just an old plate. It was my grandmother's plate, precious and unique. It deserved to be treated with a lot more respect than I had treated it. I broke it, and I did not know how to undo the damage.

Whose offering plate is it? It is the Lord's offering plate. It has, however, been placed into our hands to use as the Master would require. God trusts us with it. It is an instrument of grace paid for with the blood of Christ, God's only son. It has been taken far too lightly in the past. The offering is God's, and that makes it a BIG DEAL. We can no longer just treat it casually and with little regard. We cannot be satisfied with just doing what has been done before. We cannot continue to act like the offering plate is the intermission experience in worship. It is not your plate. It is God's plate, and it deserves all the respect we can give.

Today's plate may be an electronic draft, a website click, or a kiosk set up outside the worship center or gathering space. Any way you do it, it is still all to be done for the mission of making disciples of Jesus Christ. If we will keep our minds focused more on whose it is—and thus keep our focus on mission rather than on procedure, be it old or new—then we will do just fine. We must change the culture and old ways, but the mission remains the same. When you know that, you have conquered the first step toward a successful financial stewardship program.

....

CHAPTER ONE

How Did We Get in This Mess?

*D*r. Christopher, I have been listening to you for three hours and you have me convinced and also terribly troubled. I am a third-generation pastor. My father and my grandfather were both pastors. They were some of the finest men that I ever knew. They loved Christ, and they loved the church. I knew well many of their contemporaries, and they also were extremely fine Christian people with a desire to save souls and grow the church. They, however, were a part of the generation that has left me with a church that receives a much lower percentage of income from its members than they received. Where did they go wrong? How did we get in this mess?

I would hate to say that the grandfather and father of this pastor were all to blame for where we find ourselves today. I would never judge them or others of their generation on the commitment of their hearts or their love of the church. They operated on what they knew with the best that they knew and perhaps wondered why things did not go better. I would also point out that previous generations had their demons to fight. They were also not left with a perfect world or a perfect church, and I am sure they were trying to make adjustments in their own time with many of the changes that were called for.

The generations who led the church prior to the current one led us through the civil rights era, Vietnam protests, and the assassinations of a president, presidential candidate, and Martin Luther King, Jr. They fought through issues on women's rights, ecumenism, charismata, and Vatican II. They led the church as a president resigned and the cold war raged. Contemporary worship, the power of the Spirit, and Mormonism were hotly debated. That generation had its share of problems with a mixture of

> WE CANNOT RELY on what was said or done yesterday and expect it to be effective today.

successes and failures. They are not the issue. We are the issue. This is *our* time! It will do us little good to look back and shame those who came before. We can affect only the future from the present. So let us concentrate on what we must do now so as to not exacerbate the problem, particularly when it comes to Christian financial stewardship.

First, we must not make the mistake of General Motors. We cannot rely on what was said or done yesterday and expect it to be effective today. Just because it was right or righteous before does not necessarily make it the best course of action today. It used to be that all a mainline Protestant church had to do to grow was put a sign up in the yard announcing its presence. Not anymore. Today that church must show that it is worthy of someone getting out of bed on Sunday morning and attending. It must prove to the inquirer that one's presence there is beneficial to his or her life as compared to attending a soccer game with a child or just clicking the remote to catch Rev. Smiley and his

> **NOW, YOU MUST** not only encourage generous giving but also sell people on the fact that the place to be most generous is "God's Place."

200-piece orchestra. Your grandfather did not have to contend with those kinds of competition.

All Reverend Grandfather had to do to raise money for his church was pass the plate on Sunday morning and urge his people to be givers instead of hoarders. He never had to convince them that the church was the *best* place to give because in many instances it was the *only* place to give. Now, you must not only encourage generous giving but also sell people on the fact that the place to be most generous is "God's Place." It is a new day and requires a new message.

There is a very good possibility that your grandfather and you received the same training in stewardship and fundraising. That is, none! Pastors have often complained to me as I teach that they had no formal education in financial stewardship or fundraising, yet when they got into a church they found it was fundamental to their success. I conducted a confidential survey among about one thousand of these pastors and, indeed, 85 percent reported having no training whatsoever.

It was almost as if the seminaries assumed that monies would easily flow to the church if they would just teach their students how to preach and teach and visit. When I look at those same schools I notice that all of them have fundraising departments. They all expect the president to fundraise. They know that they must compete for funds with other schools, nonprofits, and yes, the very churches they are educating students for. Why would they not realize that those students need to be trained to do the same thing? To prevent this mess from going forward we need our professional training schools to professionally train our pastors in this vital and always necessary task of securing funds for ministry.

You and your grandfather probably both look at those you are raising funds from as "members." Most churches refer to those who have pledged some sort of allegiance to it as members. This can lead to a mind-set that is dangerous. Some people see their "membership" as entitling them to some service. People are members of country clubs or airline clubs or fraternity groups. Membership in each entitles one to certain amenities and perks. These same members can often be "made" to contribute to something with an assessment or dues to maintain membership. A country club I once belonged to decided to build a new swimming pool, and I was sent a letter telling me what my assessment was for such a project. No need to fundraise

> ## DONORS GIVE A
> lot more when they feel they are getting a lot back.

5

here. Members understood they had certain obligations, but they would benefit from getting to enjoy the new pool. That approach is not likely to work with your church "members."

For us to change the way things are, pastors and church leaders today must begin to see their "members" as "donors." Donors have a choice in what to give, when to give, and why to give. For us to pretend otherwise is foolish. These donors give a whole lot more when they feel they are getting a whole lot back. What they want is results. They want to know that from their contributions the world is being changed. They want to know that lives are being positively affected and that their gifts made a difference. If you can work on this mind-set, you will have a chance to leave a different future for your son or daughter.

....

CHAPTER TWO

Do We Really Have to Compete?

This whole idea of competing just does not seem right to me. I did not go to seminary to compete with other people doing good work. I want to work with them, not compete against them. Yes, I want to keep my church going and make it even stronger, but I don't want to compete.

The biggest transformation we have to make, it seems to me, is to learn to compete for the charitable dollar. We are consistently losing market share (a percentage of charitable dollars given), and one of the biggest reasons is that we are not making our case in a way that is convincing to the people who have dollars to give. So who loses here? I argue

NOT-FOR-PROFIT organizations are not the church. They do not have the mission of the church.

that the church is worth making a case for and what we do is unique among all other nonprofits. We have to learn to fight for the church with convincing cases, or we will soon find ourselves without a church.

This is not to say that we have to say bad things about wonderful nonprofit institutions. We should not. They are often highly effective in their area of specialization, and in many instances are doing work that our Lord wants done. No, we must help them and praise them and cooperate with them. But they are not the church. They do not have the mission of the church. So while we praise what they do we must be ready to share our stories as well and make our case as forcefully as they make theirs so donors will hopefully help us both.

The other day I was visiting with a key donor of a church along with the pastor. The pastor was asking the donor if she would be willing to serve in a very significant capacity in an upcoming campaign for their church. I fully expected the woman to say yes. She was an elected leader in the church and was the third highest donor, giving a high five-figure contribution to the operating budget each year. She was, it seemed to me on paper, an ideal candidate for the position.

> "I MUST SEE THAT my money is going to be used wisely, as God calls me to do," she said. "Is our church the best place for me to give?"

He began the conversation by bragging on her to me and then he asked her if she would be willing to consider service in this capacity. I then followed up by explaining to her what the position entailed and after about ten minutes I shut up waiting to hear her enthusiastic "Of course!" Instead, I got an answer I totally did not expect.

She looked at her pastor and said, "I am concerned about our church. For the last several years we have not grown, and I see fewer and fewer young people. I think you are a fine man, but I am beginning to wonder if supporting this church is good stewardship. Lately, I have been looking into giving more support to World Vision and Oxfam. Pastor, do you really believe that our church is a better place for my money than they are? I must see that my money is going to be used wisely, as God calls me to do. Is our church the best place for me to give? That is what I need answered because if it is not then I could not serve with integrity in the area you want me to."

The pastor, who is a very nice man, was stunned. I could see on his face that he was shocked by the request to justify to the woman why she should choose his church for her offerings. He stumbled around a bit and then turned to me to help him out. There really was nothing a person in my position could say, however. It was not my church, and I was not a leader in it. I was just a consultant. She already knew that I would play little or no role in whether this church eventually moved forward or not. I vainly tried to put a good face on what we were trying to do, but in the end she turned us down. What she ultimately decides to do with her gift will be determined by how well the church can compete for it as a place that changes lives over other very good causes.

> WE ARE THE ONE place whose mission it is to bring people into life-changing relationships with Jesus Christ.

People need to hear our life-changing stories and be helped to understand how their dollars are creating positive change in the lives of people in ways that other institutions could not do. If we want to argue that we are a great place for people to feed the hungry, then World Vision and Oxfam will beat us every day because they are experts at feeding the underprivileged. We, however, are the one place whose mission it is to bring people into life-changing relationships with Jesus Christ. Share with people how this place helps bring the power of the Holy Spirit into broken and grief-stricken lives. Point out how those who were without direction came to find that direction and a new life through the church. Compete on that field, and you will be chosen.

The persons in our pews are asking, "Why should I choose the church over World Vision or Oxfam or the Boy Scouts or the university or the hospital?" We must be prepared on a daily basis to boldly answer the question, and if we find we cannot easily do it, then we must get busy changing our church. As the builder generation dies off and is replaced by the much more discerning boomers and Gen

> TELL ME HOW YOU are changing lives and making the world a better place to live. Tell me how the dollar I give you is going to make a difference.

ONE GROUP'S GOAL is a balanced budget while the other group's goal is to change and save lives. Who do you think I want to support?

Xers, we are going to find ourselves facing that very question.

If you believe your church is truly worth supporting then be prepared to make your case to me. You do not have to say one bad thing about other places; just make sure you have a case to make about your place. Tell me how you are changing lives and making the world a better place to live. Tell me how the dollar I give you is going to make a difference. This is what I mean by compete.

Think about it. In any given week I am receiving material in the mail that tells me how the YMCA or Boys Club is changing young delinquents into responsible young people. I am getting information emphasizing the number of newborn babies saved by new technology from Children's Hospital. I am getting newsletters telling me how several of my college's recent graduates are making a real difference in society. The Red Cross is telling me how many people got pints of blood and how many are being fed after a recent hurricane. The Salvation Army is letting me know how an alcoholic is now sober and a homeless woman now has a home, all from that dollar dropped in the red kettle. Then you come along and tell me that the budget is going to increase by 4 percent this year, and you really hope I will increase my giving because not only do we need that 4 percent, but we were 5 percent short this year and really need at least 9 percent. Your goal is a balanced budget while their goal is to change and save lives. Who do you think I will want to support?

Yes, I understand that competition is not an easy concept for many a pastor or lay leader. But it better become more a part of our lives, or we will soon find ourselves far behind in the need for dollars. Even though people may still find food and shelter and healing through those other nonprofits, they will not come to know the saving grace of God through Jesus Christ. That is a case worth making!

....

CHAPTER THREE

How Do I Come Up with All These Stories?

You argue that we have to tell our stories of changing lives each week. That is 52 stories. How do I come up with these stories?

In my earlier book I shared how nonprofits are keenly aware of the number one reason why individuals choose to make a gift to an institution. It is their belief in the mission of that institution. It is their conviction that this particular place really is performing a mission that I, the donor, value and want to support. It almost always involves changing lives in some way or another. People give to homeless shelters when they see that the shelters are effectively housing the homeless and helping move many of them back into a productive life in society. They support a college when they see it graduate students and perform tasks in society that could not have been done without the college. They support a hospital when they see firsthand how lives are being saved and the sick are being made well. All of these things are what we want to see happen in our society. Since we cannot personally perform all these good works, we send money to those who are doing so.

People used to support a church just because that was one of the things "good people" did. They ate what their mother put on their plate. They had respect for their elders. They wore ties and dresses on Sunday morning and went to see Grandma afterwards. They always said "yes sir" or "no ma'am," held the door open for a lady, and only bought what was "made in America." Times have changed.

Today we live in a society that is asking

> **SHARE SPECIFICALLY** how a life has been changed directly from a relationship with your church. Share how the world has been made just a little bit better because you are in business.

why? It is not that what people used to do was bad. It may have been or may not have been. It is just that today it is challenged, and we have to be ready to defend why we believe something is correct or best. Just relying on "We've always done it this way" will not work anymore.

Most of our churches are still relying on history to fund their present ministries. They just tell people what money they need and then when they do not get it they bring down a hailstorm of guilt to try and get them to fork it over. It has not been working very well for the last fifty years, but we still keep trying the same old thing.

The church must start sharing in the same way that all non-profits do. Take your basic mission and then share experiences or stories that show you are doing exactly what people have been funding you to do. Share specifically how a life has been changed directly from a relationship with your church. Share how the world has been made just a little bit better because you are in business.

EVERY NONPROFIT I know would love to have this opportunity to speak in person with a large number of their donors every seven days, like the church does. Take advantage of it.

The ideal place to do this sharing is on Sunday mornings during worship and perhaps immediately prior to taking up the offering. Have a person who has a story to tell stand and share for no more than one or two minutes. If you have video then use that to communicate a prerecorded story. As much as possible, however, have the individual most involved in the story tell it. If a pastor says, "We have a member who . . ." it is OK but not nearly as powerful as having the actual member speak on the impact the church has had on him or her.

Every nonprofit I know would love to have this opportunity to speak in person with a large number of its donors every seven days, like the church does. Take advantage of it. People are craving to hear how you are changing lives, so tell them.

The questioner did not question the validity of what I am asking for, however, but wondered how she can acquire a new story of a changed life each week. I suspect she is looking to hit a home run every time out, and that is not practical or needed.

Yes, I hope that throughout the year every church can have stories of bringing people to Christ who did not know him and letting the congregation hear the power of that transformation, but other, less dramatic stories are perfectly valid even if they don't involve being born again. A young person sharing what it meant to go on a mission trip to Mexico—how he came to understand another culture and got to know people much less fortunate than he—is a great story. A Sunday school teacher sharing a question or comment she heard from a child can have real power. A senior adult might want to share what the support of the church meant personally during a time of grief or loss. A man may want to share what preparing the church's landscape meant to him. Another may share how a sermon affected a decision she had to make. Another might simply share what life in the church has meant in terms of friendship and support after being away from church for a long time. These are all occurrences in our churches that happen on a very regular basis. Pastors hear them all the time. From now on make a note, and as soon as you hear it mark it as a possible sharing for Sunday morning offering time.

In a large church, you can have a staff member assigned to getting the stories and prepping the speaker on how to share them on Sunday. It is a part of their job description. Smaller churches can use a volunteer to be on the lookout and do the same. Let the church know you will be doing these stories every week; if members of the congregation hear of someone or something that they feel would be inspiring, encourage them to turn it in to the proper person. Once you have gone a couple of months with these short vignettes during worship,

> **THE POWER OF** these stories is in the sharing of how your church has uniquely affected lives in a way that others could not do.

the congregation will catch on, and you will be getting calls all the time making you aware of more and more. It should be easy.

Remember, the power of these stories is in the sharing of how your church has uniquely affected lives in a way that others could not do. If all you do is get up and say, "We collected money and sent it in for hurricane relief," it will have minimal impact. Thousands of organizations collected money for hurricane relief and did it as well as you. You want this to be a story that helps people see that their church is uniquely doing its mission and lives are directly being changed because of it. When they see and understand that, you will not have to plead for extra funds. The money will flow to help you keep doing what people want to see done.

If your church has 300 or more members and you can't find 52 stories a year, you have deeper problems than financial stewardship, my friend.

....

CHAPTER FOUR

How Can I Peek?

(This chapter and the two that follow it all deal with the issue of the pastor needing to know the giving of his or her members. I considered grouping all of these into one chapter, but since they were three separate questions, I chose to break them up. Each one deals with a very different aspect of the pastor having knowledge of a member's giving history.)

I believe you when you say that all pastors should know the giving of their members, but I am serving a church that has a hard and fast rule against it. The treasurer will not let me get near those records. She said if there is something I need to

> **THE CHURCH IS**
> the only nonprofit on the
> planet that does not want
> its leader to know every-
> thing he or she can about
> how the nonprofit func-
> tions and pays its bills.

know she will inform me. I want to know, but I also do not want to tear up the church and ruin my ministry over the issue. How do I get the church to change its policy?

One of the more ridiculous policies in many of our churches has to do with this rule about the pastor not knowing what individuals in the church give. It makes absolutely no sense, yet I see one intelligent layperson after another defend this archaic policy. Frankly, I think it has no defense.

The church is the only nonprofit on the planet that does not want its leader to know everything he or she can about how the nonprofit functions and pays its bills. No college would even think of having a president who could not see what the alumni are giving. No hospital in America would have a policy that forbids its CEO from seeing what was happening with the donor base of the hospital. In fact, most of them have policies that require early and frequent acquaintance with the major donors of the nonprofit as a part of the job description. The reason is simple: the organization or institution wants to succeed in raising more funds than it raised before. Fund-raisers know that the CEO is the most important person in the fundraising process and will use that individual in every way possible.

Churches with such a policy as the one described usually are not mean-spirited. They are just not well informed about what is effective and what is not. They often are just people who inherited an ancient policy and never considered anything else. It is difficult to change, however, because people are suspicious of the motives behind seeking the change. It is a minefield that I would tread lightly around, but I would move forward seeking a change nevertheless.

The first thing I would do is assemble a couple of the leaders of the church whom you perceive are progressive, supportive, and trusting of you as their pastor. These people must also be good stewards of their finances. Share with them what you have learned about the ministry value of knowing what people are giving. Give them a copy of my book and encourage them to read it for themselves. Share with them how you would see yourself using this information and the good it would do the church in fulfilling its ministry objectives. Ask them to help you get this policy changed. Give them a couple of days to consider it, and if they are agreeable then bring a few more people into the discussion. As the circle slowly expands you can then get official permission, and the treasurer should be informed.

I would not then make a big deal out of the change. It really is not a big deal, and Armageddon will not occur. It is a mistake to go out on a Sunday morning and make an announcement or use the pastor's column to tell people you are looking. That is just dumb. You have been handed a ministry tool to serve your church. Treat it like that and move on.

Don't think I am naive about this. I know that some people can and will make a big deal out of it. If, however, you have quietly built a base of support from your leaders, they will put the ya-ya down and you can go about your business. You will have done your ministry a big favor, and you also will have helped all ministers who might

> BE SURE THAT your leaders understand that your knowledge of giving is a spiritual diagnostic tool that you must have to be effective in dealing with persons' souls, and in being a faithful leader.

follow you. They will not have to fight the battle that you just won.

The key to your success on this is to keep the discussion on a ministry plane. Be sure that your leaders understand that your knowledge of giving is a spiritual diagnostic tool that you must have to be effective in dealing with persons' souls and in helping the church have the most effective leadership possible. Be alert, however, that one or two of your trusted leaders may not be giving as they should and do not want you to know it. They will quietly sabotage this under the guise of serving the church. Do your best to ascertain that those whom you seek out early on are exemplary stewards to the church.

Lots of things in ministry are tough and will get you questioned. Why did you choose to visit this person instead of that person? You should go and visit anyway. Why did you preach that sermon on that Sunday instead of this sermon on that Sunday? Preach your sermon anyway. Why did you write that article in the newsletter instead of another article? Write it anyway, IF YOU FEEL THAT IT IS WHAT THE LORD WANTS YOU TO DO. This must be your motivation in changing this policy or anything else you want to do in your church. Help people see the rationale of why the Lord is encouraging you to lead as you are leading and you should be fine. Make it personal and you will fail.

Finally, let me add that this is not something that you should "go to Jerusalem" over. Jesus did not ride into Jerusalem until the issue at hand was worth taking nails over. This is not one of those issues. It is the most discussed of all my recommendations and the one that seems to get both preachers and laity all in a tizzy. It is important, but it is not worth losing a ministry over or tearing up a church for. This is a discussion worth having and a policy worth changing, but I would not go to war over it.

CHAPTER FIVE

Won't It Hurt My Eyes or My Heart?

I *have been a minister for more than twenty years, and I have never chosen to know who gives what to the budget of the church. I have told my congregations from the beginning that I did not know and did not want to know. I really don't want to know because I am afraid of what it may do to me. I know that when I see that a person I have been counting on to lead in the church is a poor giver, it will affect my relationship with them. I know that I will probably consider who is giving when I choose people for certain positions. I don't want to show favoritism. Is it wrong to feel that you should treat your members equally?*

CHOOSING NOT TO know what our members give constitutes clergy malpractice.

Research has shown that about one-third of all clergy know what their members are giving. The two-thirds who do not know are equally divided between churches that have rules against it and pastors who have a personal rule against it. The previous question came from a pastor serving a church that will not let him know who gives. This question comes from a pastor who may well have served churches that would allow her to see, but she afraid to do so for fear of it influencing her relationship with a member or changing how she might minister to someone. Frankly, I think it has come about more as a defensive position than a ministry position. Most pastors know that the safe route is to not know, thus preventing anyone from suggesting that the pastor is "only pastoring the money" or "favoring the rich."

Choosing not to know what our members are giving constitutes clergy malpractice. It is malpractice because the clergyperson is denying himself or herself access to a diagnostic tool that can tell us a great deal about the soul of the donor. It would be malpractice just as if a doctor failed to order an X-ray for a mangled arm because he was afraid someone might question the cost of the proce-

> YOU CAN'T LOVE
>
> Jesus and not
>
> be generous.

dure. It is well known among doctors and almost everyone that an arm that is twisted awkwardly is probably broken and an X-ray is needed to confirm it. To not do one would be considered medical malpractice almost everywhere. It is equally well known that how one gives is one of the best indicators of the condition of a person's soul. Being a generous person is not a fool-proof indicator that his or her soul is secure with the Lord, but if the person is not giving, you can just about take it to the bank that Jesus Christ is not Lord of his or her life. You can't love Jesus and not be generous. The job of every clergyperson is helping people grow in relationship to Christ. Denying oneself access to the single greatest tool to assist you in making a spiritual diagnosis is then clergy malpractice.

To the pastor asking this question I say that, yes, it will affect your relationship with the person. It should. It should affect your relationship with the person whether they are giving or not giving. Your relationship with them should be different because you know that THEY ARE DIFFERENT.

LEADERS IN THE church must, by their actions, exemplify the life Christ called for. Generosity is one of the traits of that life.

When you have a member that is showing extreme generosity, is involved in serving the community, is present each week for worship, and has an active devotional life, then you have a member that, from all measurable points, has a close walk with Jesus. He or she should be treated differently than a member who does not exhibit these characteristics. A competent pastor should plan strategies with each individual, designed to help him or her along on the spiritual journey. Individuals are thus treated differently. However, they should not be *loved* differently. In fact, one of the most loving things you could do with the nongiver is help him or her learn the value of generosity and get free of the bondage of stuff.

I love my children. My wife and I share four of them. They are all precious to us. They are all, however, very different. Only one of our children has children. Because of that, one of their greatest needs is for Grandmother and I to babysit and free Mom and Dad up for a night out. It is a way we can love them. None of the other three needs us to come and sit in their homes for an extended period on a Saturday night. Another of our children lives more than a thousand miles away. It helps him a lot if, on occasion, we can spring for an airline ticket so he can come see members of the family. Another child lives twenty miles away and would not be particularly helped by our paying transportation cost for her to come see us. We love them all, but we show how we love them differently.

Most pastors know these things but have a hard time applying them to finances. Money is the great untouchable in our congregations and thus most pastors just stay away from it. When I hear pastors saying that they want to treat their members equally, I know they do not really mean it. Pastors make decisions every day about who to visit and not visit. They just don't want to ever think that money was a part of the equation in determining that visit.

How persons give should be at the top of the page for every pastor in determining his or her priorities in ministry just about

KNOWING HOW YOUR members are giving should play a role in helping you determine what to preach on, and how to address the role of money in people's lives.

WHY WOULD YOU want to know about so many things going on in a person's walk with Christ, but not this one? every day. When it comes to selecting people to serve in leadership in the church you must have people who, by their actions, are exemplifying the life that Christ called for, and generosity certainly was one of those traits. When seeking to determine what homes to visit that week, why would you not want to include a visit or two to persons not giving so as to ascertain the conditions of their souls? Not giving is a symptom of a sick souls and you are the soul doctor. Knowing how your members are giving should play a role in helping you determine what to preach on a given Sunday and exactly how to address the issue of the role of money in people's lives.

Do you want to know who attends worship and who does not? Do you want to know who is going on a mission trip and who is not? Do you want to know who is singing in the choir and who is teaching Sunday school? I hope so, because you need to know who your spiritual giants are so that they might lead others into the life abundant.

Do you want to know which of your families are going through marital crisis? Do you want to identify any youth who may be on

> OUR JOB AS pastors is to know about money so we can help our people have life and have it abundantly.

drugs or participating in harmful sexual behavior? Is it just so you can gossip about town? I hope not. I hope the answer to all those questions is a resounding yes because you care about the souls of those persons and you want them to have a fulfilling life now and everlasting. You know that marital infidelity, drugs, and promiscuous sex can lead more to death than to life.

So explain to me again why you would not want to know about the one behavior (generosity) that when done correctly brings peace, joy, happiness, and contentment? Why would you not want to know about the behavior that when done poorly can lead to a life of frustration, bewilderment, idolatry, and confusion?

Our job as pastors is not to know about money for money's sake. Our job is to know about money so we can help our people have life and have it abundantly. You owe it to your people to know everything about them that you can, so you can treat each and every one as an individual child of God, unique in his or her own way (both good and bad). Only in doing so can you then help them to begin to be all that their heavenly Father created them to be.

....

CHAPTER SIX

What Do I Look for
When I Look?

*O*K, *I am convinced that I need to be reviewing the giving records of my members. I am not excited about it
because I know it is going to wound my soul. I want
to believe the best about my people and this may reveal a hypocrite
or two that I don't want to know about. Anyway, I am going to
do it. What do I need to be looking for?*

I know how you feel. I remember when I first came out of
seminary and believed that all the people who went to my
church loved Jesus. It did not take too long for that bubble
to burst. I also thought they had the church's best interest at
heart and later found out that, for many, the church was

> YOU ARE NOT and will never be in the money business. You are in the ministry and mission business.

simply a way for them to care for their own self interest. Hey, nobody said that being a pastor was going to be easy. You are called to preach against sin to a bunch of sinners who don't want you to preach on their particular sin. You are called to preach "from the Bible" to a group of people who hardly ever open theirs. You are called to run a very complicated nonprofit organization with an often blurry mission, with your success dependent upon a collection of volunteers that you cannot fire or even hold accountable. It is a tough job and knowing what people are giving can break your heart, but it can also make your day. Absolutely nothing else comes close to revealing to you what is the true nature of someone's soul.

It is extremely important for you to always remember your mission, especially when it comes to reviewing finances. You are not and will never be in the money business. You are in the ministry and mission business. Your top priority is not to achieve a certain cash flow or credit/debit percentage. Your job at the end of the day is to save and care for souls. Your every reason to review the individual giving records is to enlighten you on how might be the best way to accomplish that mission.

You want to look for change first of all. If someone has been giving at a certain level for some time and that changes, then you can bet something has occurred in that person's life. Has there been a job loss or maybe a promotion? Has there been a family crisis of some sort that has caused the change? Has the person undergone a spiritual experience that has brought about a change in the way he or she manages money? Are they struggling with something going on in the church family that you might help with?

I used to make a record of what families were giving before and after being exposed to a growth class or retreat experience. It was a magnificent way to test the effectiveness of a new program. If a certain multiple-week Bible study did not produce any change in how people gave, then I had to wonder if it was all that effective. I would have assumed that if the study genuinely touched their hearts to the point that serving Jesus became a higher priority in

WHEN A LARGE gift shows up, send the giver a note to thank them.

> **THE IDEA IS** to be disciplined in thanking three or four people for their financial giving each week. Then do six or seven more notes thanking people for things other than financial giving.

their lives, I would see some evidence in their giving. If I saw it then I would make a note to repeat the study for others. If I did not I might reevaluate and use something different next time.

You will also want to be alert to first-time donors. If someone started coming to the church just two Sundays ago and I saw that they gave generously both Sundays, I would send a personal thank you and also follow up to see what their Christian background was. It was obvious from their giving that participation in the faith was not a new thing for this family, and I need to be aware of how they might quickly be used in leadership at the church. They would need that invitation, and the church could use their involvement. I would always tell my treasurer to flag these families and gifts for me so I would not miss them in my review.

You should be looking for three or four donors each week to send thank you notes to. You will want to send one to

Tom & Mike could provide

someone who has recently shown a significant increase in his or her regular offering. Let that person know you noticed and appreciate his or her support. Send one to someone who appears to have dropped a large one-time gift in the plate. People get bonuses in their work, inherit funds, sell properties, or other situations where they have extra ability, and they made a choice to share that with the church and their Lord. When you see a gift like that, send a note and thank the donor. If you don't see any gifts like these then just choose one of the faithful regular giving families and send them a note. The idea is to be disciplined in thanking three or four people for their financial giving each week. Then do six or seven more notes thanking people for things other than financial giving.

Your observations will often lead to visits. You might see that someone has started consistently giving less but you do not know why. Go see them. Early in the visit tell them what you saw and make them aware that often that is a sign of a problem in the household and you wanted to see if there was any way you could be helpful. Your communication is that you care about THEM and THEIR SOULS, not the offering amount. Such a visit is frequently the impetus for someone to make you aware of a serious need in his or her life.

Visits also need to be made to those persons who show sizeable giving increases. Again the concern here in thanking them is not so you can keep the dollars flowing in, but so you can ascertain if something has occurred in their lives that can enrich the church body. Do they have testimonies they might share? Do they need to be used in leadership positions to encourage others to be generous? Once again, you begin this visit by sharing what you have observed and asking the family or person to share what is behind the change. Then you evaluate how best to use the information.

....

CHAPTER SEVEN

What Did You Mean About Lay Leaders Having Access to Giving Records?

I *have always had access to individual giving records as you encourage and this has not been any problem in any church I served. However, I heard you say that lay leaders should also have access. I have never done this and am not sure I understand what you mean. Are we to publish giving records on the doorpost? Who exactly do you mean? Could you explain the rationale a bit more for me?*

This gets into that same tricky area of money being sort of taboo to mention in public or in the church. People's salaries are not to be spread about for all to see, but they are known by those who have a need to know. What people give is to be treated confidentially as well, but it should be known by those who have a need to know.

My wife was a school teacher for a number of years. Her salary at the school was set each year. It was not printed in the daily newspaper, but it was certainly known by everyone who was on the school board. To do their jobs properly they needed to have a clear understanding of where their money was coming from and where it was going.

Last year I refinanced the loan on my house. The lending institution asked and received a copy of my W2 so the loan officer could see exactly what I was being paid. Again, it was not printed for everyone in the community to see, but I understood that the lenders had to have that salary information in order

> IT IS FOOLISH for us to expect the congregation's leaders to make the best decisions on behalf of the Lord they serve without having access to all the information necessary.

for them to do their jobs.

Our board leaders, deacons, finance committee members, stewardship chairs, and others are charged with making decisions that have serious impact on the body of Christ.

WOULD YOU WANT to accept a position where you are held accountable for outcomes, yet you were not given all the information necessary to make good decisions? Yet church after church is run this way.

Frankly, as an aside, I think those decisions are more important than those made by a lending institution or public school. Anyway, it is foolish for us to expect these leaders to make the best decisions on behalf of the Lord they serve without having access to all the information necessary. Specific information about how income flows into the church can influence a decision and keep a church from making a mistake. We should not only allow it but require it. Does God talk only to the treasurer? Is it wise to just let that person do all of the financial interpretation for us? Does God talk only to the pastor? Should we make that person solely responsible to interpret cash flow for the entire church? I surely would not want to accept a position of responsibility where someone might be able to hold me accountable for outcomes when I did not have all the information possible available to me. Yet church after church is run this way.

A part of the defense of those persons who were top officers of Enron and Worldcom and Tyco was that they really did not know what was going on and thus should not be held accountable. They blamed the wrongs on persons in lesser positions who just did not do their jobs well. In case after case juries said that was nonsense. As corporate officers they were responsible, and if they did not know then they should have known. Many of those people are serving significant prison time today. Yet, church after church after church is being run just like these failed corporations. Financial information is not in the hands of those making important decisions. A part of that information has to do with cash flow, and that has to

> UPON REVIEWING individual giving, I have discovered many things that would have a profound effect on decisions I recommend to a church. Would it not also be wise for the leaders within that church to have the same information?

do with individual donors. For the finance chairperson, ruling body chairperson, head deacon, or whomever to truly be able to advise and assist the pastor they need access.

A year ago, I was studying a church's potential to achieve a certain target in a capital campaign. The lay leader who contacted me told me all the basic stuff like the size of the budget and last year's income, amount of the debt, what the project was going to cost, and size of the church. He also said he knew the number of donor families if that would help and told me it was 362. He said he did not have any individual information but hoped that would be enough for me to help his committee decide. I contacted the pastor to see about getting individual giving records. He said he did not have access but would ask the treasurer. The treasurer was very hesitant but finally agreed to send me a list of the top ten donors and what they gave.

Right at the top was a name and an amount of giving that represented 42 percent of the church's income. One family was supporting 42 percent and only the treasurer and I knew it. I contacted this gentleman, and we had a very pleasant discussion. During the discussion he explained to me why he was absolutely and unequivocally opposed to this project and would not be giving to it. He was not going to make a big deal out of it and wished the church well, but it simply would not be a priority for him.

Now, any businessman seeking to forecast a business decision who sees that the decision will not be supported by a customer who represents 42 percent of his revenue would probably want to factor that fact into the equation of whether to go forward or not. But these church leaders were absolutely blind to this reality. Is that a good way to run a church, or anything for that matter? Does keeping this known only to a treasurer who feels bound to total silence advance the mission at all?

I don't often see churches with one person giving 42 percent, but I have seen more than one, and I have seen numerous ones where fewer than ten families contributed 50 percent or more of the church budget. I have also seen churches where giving was remarkably even across the board for reasons still unknown to me. In other words, when I have examined individual giving I have discovered many things that would have a profound effect on decisions I recommend to a church. Would it not also be wise for the leaders within that church to have the same information?

I would have a church policy that stated clearly who has access to individual records and always for only one purpose—to assist the pastor in making decisions on behalf of the church.

....

CHAPTER EIGHT

Do We Tell When Things Are Bad?

*I*n reading your book I noted that it is important to communicate that the leaders of the church are being fiscally responsible. Do we not even tell the congregation when things are going badly and we are running a deficit? Do we just put on a Pollyanna smile and hope for the best?

It is important that we communicate to the congregation that we are being fiscally responsible, or a better way to put it is to say we have been faithful stewards. One of the top factors for a donor in choosing to make a gift is confidence that the nonprofit is fiscally sound and responsible. No donor likes the idea that the gift he or she gives is just

> **THE CHURCH IS**
> the only nonprofit entity
> that believes crying wolf
> and showing people
> that you don't have
> enough money to
> perform your mission is
> an intelligent way to raise
> funds. It is not!

plugging a hole in a sinking ship. Year after year people show by their giving that they will support strong charities that demonstrate that they have used gifts wisely and for the causes to which those gifts were given.

No nonprofit that I have ever been associated with would even think of airing its dirty laundry for all its donors to see. When donors get a whiff of an institution that is in serious financial trouble they do not rush over with their checkbooks. They start looking for another institution to fund. Therefore, when an institution is having financial difficulties (and they do), they work diligently on the problems within the board and do not broadly air them out for all the community of donors to hear.

This whole line of thinking gets at the root of charitable giving today. Donors do not wish to prop up institutions of any kind, but they aspire to make the world a better place to live. People want to give to programs that are changing lives. Nobody supports the Red Cross because it has a big cross for a sign and neat, white trucks that roam around our towns. They support the Red Cross because they have seen it changing lives after earthquakes, hurricanes, fires, and in operating rooms. They aren't supporting an institution but a change agent. Words about financial distress to prop up an institution would be a death blow to this proud servant group. Like most all successful nonprofits, it keeps financial information within the board room and life-changing information out in front of its donors.

The church continues to be the only nonprofit entity that believes crying wolf and showing people that you don't have enough money to perform your mission is an intelligent way to raise funds. It is not!

What I argued for in *Not Your Parents' Offering Plate* was not for anyone to be dishonest in their reporting to the congregation but, in most instances, be more honest so as to reflect that good stewardship is being practiced.

For instance, it has become a bad habit

> **WHEN I READ**
> biblical stories of God's people at worship, I just do not see anywhere that a financial report is included.

for churches to publish financial information in the worship bulletin or church newsletter. Ninety percent of the time this will show that the church is running a deficit for the year. The reason is that the finance committee simply divides the budget by 52 and reports to the congregation as if funds arrive in equal installments each week. The vast majority of churches receive their largest gifts in December. By the end of December they have raised the funds needed to fund the ministries budgeted for. However, at the end of November they are behind. Let's be honest with our congregations and not lead them to believe that halfway through the year we expect half of our income. Saying so leaves an impression that we are not good stewards, which causes income to drop, not grow.

Another cardinal sin to me is having someone use worship time to give a financial report (which is almost always negative). When I review the Psalms and other references to Old Testament and New Testament worship, I just do not see anywhere that a financial report is included. As I visit various worship services around the country this is one of the greatest turnoffs to my worship experience. No one, and I mean no one, comes to a worship service to hear whether the budget is balanced or not. They have come to touch the face of God. Never do anything that makes that harder to do.

One Sunday while out of town conducting one of my seminars I decided to attend a church not far from the hotel where I was staying. It had an interesting exterior and a fairly modern sign, both of which attracted me to choose it for worship that day. I checked on the time of worship with an internet search and got there about ten minutes early. Upon entering what seemed to be the main worship center entrance, I received a bulletin and headed for a seat on the aisle about halfway down. The place was not one-third full at that time. Seating was easy. By my watch it was about one minute until worship was to start, and I began to fidget a bit wondering if something was wrong. Absolutely no life could be seen or heard from the chancel dealing with the worship of God. However, within a minute the organist and a piano player arrived to take their seats. They played for about forty-five seconds and then a choir began to process in. Behind them came the pastor. They approached the chancel and took their seats. Another man in a suit then went and sat down by the pastor. When the organist stopped, the man in the suit stood up and went to the pulpit. I was then ready to worship.

> DID ANYTHING happen to make me want to return and maybe be a part of this church and maybe give my tithe to this church to help it meet its obligations? NO!

"My name is John Smith" (my name for him, not his name), he began. "I am the chairman of the finance committee. I want to share some serious news with you this morning, and I hope it will be the last time I have to do this. We are currently behind our budget by about $70,000. Giving has been off for most of the year, and it seems we are in a trend that is not good. We have instructed our pastor to delete one staff person, and we have cut our ministries program budget by 10 percent. Both of these changes will help us, but we also need more money each Sunday. We hope many of you can give a bit more for the remainder of the year, and if you do we will be able to balance the budget.

"We are very appreciative of the pastor and his staff who are seeking to make do with as little as possible. They have assured us that they will not be asking for additional funds next year so we will not be asking you for more again later. We know that everyone is doing all they can, and we hate to ask you to consider anything else, but we just had no other choice. If you can help just a little we will not have to talk about money any more the rest of the year, I promise. Thank you." He then went to sit down, and the pastor stood and led a call to worship.

What do you think is all I thought about for the entire hour? What do you think the rest of the congregation thought about for that hour? Were we raised up from our weekly labors by the redeeming grace of God? Were we reminded that even in our darkest hours God's light will shine? Were we humbled by God's power in the face of our weaknesses? Were we transformed from our earthly woes to a heavenly place where tears will never flow? Were we released from the bonds of Good Friday by the resurrected power of Easter Sunday? No, we got a depressing financial report and a half-baked apology for having to make it. Did anything happen to make me want to return and maybe be a part of this church and maybe give my tithe to this church to help it meet its obligations? NO!

So when there is a real deficit or serious

> IT IS AS IF somewhere they read where Jesus said, "Go forth and balance the budget."

> **AS SOON AS** money becomes the mission then the church ceases to be the church.

financial shortfall how do you communicate it? You do it in a private communiqué to just your members and you avoid public pronouncements. You can send out an e-mail or a letter to just your people letting them know the facts and also helping them understand why this has happened. Many churches send out distress calls but never answer why a finance team and pastor approved a budget that could not be met. If you cannot readily explain how it happened you leave yourself open to rumors of impropriety or ignorance, neither of which instills confidence in the hoped-for donor. It is also important to include in the message a reminder of how you are continuing to do your mission and change lives. Ultimately, that will be what causes one to give—not just the fact that you need money now.

Here is a sample letter one could adopt when there is a real need to inform the congregation of a financial shortfall. Later on I will address the notion that these letters should be tailor-made for the donor type (tither, consistent giver, sometimes giver, and nongiver). For now, it may be helpful for you to see what a general letter addressing this issue might look like.

Dear _____, (make as personal as possible)

We are in the midst of amazing times. We watch daily as our nation wages war in the Middle East, defends against terror attacks here at home, looks for answers to such intractable problems as unemployment, poverty, and hunger, and sees retirement portfolios crash, rise, and then slide again. It can leave any of us a bit wobbly and unsteady. In the midst of these troubles your church has sought to be a bulwark never failing, reminding persons of Easter faith, and a hope that is always present. We know that this still is our Father's world.

At Grace Church we have increased our ministry with those affected by the economy. Job fairs, job-seeking seminars, financial training classes, and numerous pastoral counseling sessions have all been held. Your staff and I meet with six of our lay leaders each week on Monday to specifically pray for those going through these tough times. We are constant in seeking ways our church can and should be in ministry. The sermon series "Lilies of the Field—What, Me Worry?" has helped worship attendance rise by 30 percent as countless people from our community have joined us to learn how to cope in troubling times. It was in times like these that the church was born, and it is in times like these when people look away from idols and come to Christ. We will continue to offer Good News every day.

You should know that as these ministry needs have been pressed upon us, many of our members have been unable to fulfill their financial commitments to the church. Some have moved away to find work. Others have undergone a financial setback and had to cut back on many planned expenses. Some are just behind and are trying to catch up. We are committed to not reducing our outreach or ministry plans, if at all possible, but we need your help.

If you are able and have been blessed, even as others have suffered, I hope you will consider a special gift to your church to help us get through these days effectively. Right now it appears that we will be $100,000 short of our needs at year end. Your response can occur in two ways. You can make a one-time offering this coming Sunday, October 2, or you can place the enclosed card in the plate on that day advising us of your intention to give a certain extra amount before the year ends. Either way will help insure we continue to serve those who need us without interruption.

Last week one of our Sunday school teachers, Ed Jones, shared with me what 9-year-old Ashley Smith said after class: "Mr. Ed, it has been hard on us ever since Daddy went off to the war. My sister and I miss him and so does Mommy. Can the church just be my Daddy while he is gone, please?"

Ashley, you can count on me, and you can count on this church. We won't ever replace your Daddy, but we will be your family now and forever, even after his return. How neat it is to be in a church where little children know they can count on us.

God bless you,

Pastor _____

Now let me add a word about balancing the budget. Over the last few years I have had numerous calls from churches wanting help with balancing the budget. As I talk with them it seems that their entire ministry focus is

> **YOUR FIRST** concern should be on how you are making disciples for Christ; that should lead off every business session.

on balancing the budget. It is as if somewhere they read where Jesus said, "Go forth and balance the budget." Finance leaders have said that they just should not do anything until they balance the budget. I was actually in a church a few weeks ago where the finance chairman announced to the congregation that the finance committee had held long meetings and cut the budget painfully, but it was now balanced. The congregation applauded. Were the people happy that items were cut? Maybe we should see what else we can eliminate and make them even happier next week. This particular church gives on average about 30 percent less than similar churches in their denomination.

I wondered if they would have applauded like that if an announcement was made that a new soul had been saved or that ten new persons were baptized. I wondered if they would have applauded if two of their young people had announced they were going into ministry. Then I found myself questioning whether those things would have occurred if as much energy had been given to making them happen as went into balancing the budget.

Do not lose focus on your mission, lest you suddenly wake up and discover that balancing the budget has become your mission. For instance, do not let the finance report be the first report given in your business meetings. Your first concern should be on how you are making disciples for Christ, and that should lead off every business session. That is why you are in business! The day McDonald's ceases to concentrate on making hamburgers and only thinks about making a dollar will be the first day of the company's demise. As soon as Toyota starts to think only about the bottom line and not how to make a better car you will start to see them fail. As soon as money becomes the mission then the church ceases to be the church.

....

CHAPTER NINE

What Do Those
Letters Look Like?

*I*t never dawned on me to send a different letter out to different donors in my church. I have always just done one for the entire congregation, as if they were all just alike. Of course, I know they are not alike, and now I know they do not think alike when it comes to donation decisions. You talk about generational letters and also donor-type letters in the book. Can you give me some examples?

It always struck me as odd that my college would send out a different letter to its graduates depending upon when they graduated whereas my church always sent the same letter to everyone. The college knew that someone who

CHURCHES USUALLY send the same "we need money now" letter to those who tithe and those who haven't given to the church in twenty years.

graduated in 1950 and had been retired for several years had a different memory and understanding of the college than someone who graduated in 2000. It also knew that even though both graduated from the same institution and probably both had great affection for that institution their abilities to give were probably not similar at all. Thus the college frequently sent out letters targeted just for certain alumni groups. The reason for it was simple: the college wanted more money.

I also noticed that it made appeals differently depending upon how one had given in the past. For a person who had been a significant benefactor, owned their own company, and frequently came back for alumni functions, the college had a certain gift appeal process. For someone who had never given and hadn't been back since graduation day, the college had a very different procedure. The church, I noted, usually sent the same "we need money now" letter to the tither and to the family who had not sent in a gift in twenty years.

I frequently field phone calls from pastors wanting me to send them samples of such letters, and it always surprises me. There is nothing difficult or complicated about them. The biggest reason that most pastors don't send them has nothing to do with knowing what to write; it is just taking the time to actually do more than one letter. Regardless, I am happy to supply a few sample letters for you to see how easy it really is.

All letters for additional income need to share how the problem came about so that donors can see that the church has not been practicing fiscal irresponsibility. Each letter must also make a specific request and tell the donor how and when help is needed. Each of these letters should have a cover letter with a testimony from someone sharing how the church changed his or her life.

Letter to those over 70: this group is
responsibility/duty bound.

Dear _____, (Personalize all letters unless
absolutely impossible)

Our church, First Church of the City, has been serving our community for more than 76 years. During
that time we have stood strong in the face of hot and
cold wars, recessions, natural disasters, 13 presidents,
and 27 pastors. The year ahead should be no different
as we continue ministry to all who come our way.

Right now we need your help. Our operating
budget is experiencing quite a strain. For the year we
are down about 10 percent. Much of this is due to
some unexpected deaths and a few of our families who
have been hit hard by the economic crisis. If this continues we will fall short by about $80,000 and some of
our important ministries will suffer. It may be a strug-
gle to satisfy our conference obligations, and this
church has never failed to live up to our responsibilities there. We still have time to keep our record spot-
less and finish strong, but we will need the help or our
faithful members.

If you have been giving regularly, would you see if the year's end offers you any chance for an extra gift? If you are behind on your pledge, would you try to catch up? If you have not yet begun to give, could you remember us this week with a generous offering? Together we can come through this crisis and be stronger than ever. A response card is enclosed for you to share with us how you choose to respond. We will be announcing the total response to the congregation in two weeks.

God bless you for your continued love of your church.

Pastor _____

I am not at all a big fan of financial stewardship letters coming from the finance committee. I think they need to come from a real person, and the pastor is the best person. Finances are spiritual matters, just like asking for additional prayers. Separating financial requests from other requests sends a bad signal.

Letter to those 45-69: this group must be convinced to give.

Dear _____,

I thought you would be interested in this story about how one of our families was served by the church during a very stressful time. I appreciate their willingness to share their experience.

Almost every day we have people hurting, scared, bewildered, or just anxious coming through our doors. They come because they know this is a safe place where people will love them as Christ loves them. Hopefully, they leave a little stronger, with a little more hope, and an understanding of how their lives fit in God's grand plan.

As we approach the end of the year my prayer is that each family will faithfully review its level of financial giving to the church and do all God calls it to do to help make the church even stronger. With the economy hurting some of our families, we find ourselves about 10 percent short of meeting all of our budget needs. We need you more than ever. Could you use the enclosed response card to make an extra end-of-the-year contribution? I will be announcing in two weeks what the response of our congregation has been to this need.

Please let me know how I can serve you or your family. That is what we do. Thank you for supporting us in ways that let us share God's amazing love to more and more.

Pastor _____

Letter to 30-45 year olds:
this group responds to specifics

Dear _____,

I thought you might enjoy this story about one of our young children.

Children are the lifeblood of this church. Every day we seek to discover new and innovative ways to bring the values of faith and love into their lives. Nothing is more valued than helping one of our young ones discover God's love for them in a meaningful way.

We had 200 in VBS this year, more than 300 in Upward Basketball, and 145 on average for Sunday school. Thirty-two of our children worked in a soup kitchen over the Christmas holidays. These children are growing into the likeness of Christ.

Thank you for supporting your church so we can help our children grow. As our year ends, we'd like to get your help in purchasing a new van for our children's ministry. We have been offered a special deal for a wonderful 15-passenger van for $22,000. This passenger van will let us more safely and conveniently transport our children to church-sponsored activities (like the soup kitchen). Can you help with a one-time gift to help us purchase this van by the end of the month? We have enclosed a special response card and envelope for you to use to indicate how you might help. We will be sharing two Sundays from now what the response has been.

God bless you, and God bless our kids.

Pastor _____

Letter to 20-29 year olds: this group needs coaxing

Dear _____,

You might like this story that came from one of our college students.

Sometimes there seem to be so many changes and so many issues for one to have to deal with. The college years leading to young adulthood are full of transitions regarding work life, family life, financial life, and spiritual life. We hope as your church that we can be a positive factor in providing direction with all of these forces.

In this year alone we are offering resume classes, marriage and financial management classes, and numerous Bible classes (even for the biblical newcomer), and mission opportunities. If you don't see something that you think you need, let me know and hopefully we can get it also.

A part of that "growing" process is learning how to give as a mature Christian. I am hosting a dessert gathering at my home to discuss this aspect of our lives on Friday, November 10. This meeting is just for persons in their twenties (or close). I sincerely hope you will come and join us. The food will be extraordinary and the fellowship friendly and inviting.

Just return the self-addressed stamped card or e-mail me at pastor@church.org and let me know you are coming. I look forward to seeing you.

Pastor _____

At the house meeting you would give each one a response instrument and share how he or she can get it in and become one of the supporting families of the church.

The letters that I think should be followed most closely, however, deal more with donor types rather than with generational types. A fully committed thirty-year-old Christian tither has a lot in common with a sixty-year-old Christian tither. Following are some examples you might consider to donors with similar histories.

A letter to the tithers
(The easiest way to get a list is to have people
self-identify by signing up or checking a box on a card)

Dear _____,

Thank you, _____ (personalize as much as possible), for your faithful support of God's work through our church. You continue to lead the way in giving by being a loyal and committed tither. I thank God for you on a regular basis.

As I am sure you know, tithers are not a majority but very much a minority in the Christian world. You are one of the few who regularly practice this biblical model of giving. Years ago, I too became a tither, and it has been one of the great joys of my life. Knowing you are with me is a wonderful feeling. Together I hope we can lead more and more people to understand the blessing of this spiritual discipline.

I hope you find great joy in knowing that your giving is helping bring others to Christ, feed the hungry, educate our children, and bring hope to the hopeless. Without people like you it could not be done.

Please let me know how I can ever be of service to

you. You have been a blessing to me. Thank you, again.

Pastor _____

P.S. Your commitment card for this year's campaign is enclosed. Be sure to check the box for tithers if you are continuing your current practice of this discipline. I will call for cards to come forward this Sunday in worship.

A letter to regular givers who are not yet tithers.

Dear _____,

Over the last several years you have been a family who has consistently supported Christ's work through our church. I am thankful for you and for your support.

Your support has helped the church do some remarkable things:

(List recent ministries or accomplishments)

We want to do much more. My dreams are that soon we will be able to:

(List ministries you hope to start soon)

I want to invite you to be one of those leaders who make these dreams come true. I invite you to move up to being a tither. I have been a tither for ____ years and currently ____ families of our church are faithful practitioners of this biblical call. Is it time for you to make that step? The blessing you will receive is beyond anything I can describe. But if you try tithing for six months and find out it is not working for you, then you can have your old life back! My goal in our upcoming campaign is to double the number of tithers in our church from ____ to ____. I hope you will be one of these. I would love to visit with you and pray with you about this spiritual discipline. Please contact me so we can arrange a convenient time.

You are a great blessing, and it is a joy to be your pastor.

Pastor _____

P.S. This year's commitment card is enclosed. There is a box on it for you to check if your commitment this year moves you up to being a tither. If you are already tithing, be sure to check the box so we can add you to our list. The cards will be brought in this Sunday in worship.

For nongivers

Dear _____,

Would you consider joining those families who give regularly to our church? Currently ____ percent of our church families give to the church. Their giving allows us to:

(List recent ministries or accomplishments)

My goal for next year is to have ____ percent in our church giving. My invitation to you is to set a target of $5 a week or $260 a year. This is less than a movie ticket and most fast food meals. However, it will make a big difference in our church when combined with others. Next year we hope to:

(List ministries you hope to start soon)

You can be a part of making great things happen with just $5 a week. Will you please consider this step and let me know your decision using the enclosed card? Families will be bringing these cards forward Sunday or mailing them in this week.

I am eager to visit with you about this decision or about anything in your life. Please do not hesitate to contact me at any time.

Pastor _____

You may want to spend a bit more time and divide your congregation up a couple of more times. This will only help.

Remember: personalize everything you can and even add a handwritten note on the bottom of many of these that shows you know this family. Also, when the cards are in be sure to send a target group specific thank you notes.

....

CHAPTER TEN

How Do I Ask for Capital When I Am Not in a Capital Campaign?

Clif, I just do not know how I can be asking for a capital gift when my church is not in a capital campaign. It was not a problem when we were building our educational building two years ago. What am I to do today?

One of the arguments that I made in my previous book dealt with how every donor in the church has three pockets to give from. There is the annual pocket (earned income), the capital pocket (generally accumulated wealth not

> CAPITAL GIFTS should not fund buildings but rather a vision of greater ministry.

associated with every day cash flow), and the planned pocket (estate gifts). Every nonprofit I have ever been associated with seeks gifts from all three of these pockets every year. By and large, though, the church does not. We regularly ask in our offering time for the annual pocket, but only about 5 percent seek the planned gift, and very few seem to care about a capital gift except during the time a building is being considered. What this does is abdicate this gift to the college, hospital, or other nonprofit who smartly communicates to the donor about ways it could use it.

First, our thinking must change on what capital gifts do. They should not be funding buildings but funding a vision of greater ministry. Capital gifts fund the dreams of the disciples who are always looking forward to consider how they might do more if only funds were available. It is this vision and these dreams that always need to be before the people. Way too often, I see churches and pastors who seem to have Ferris wheel vision. When they need a building they are at the top of the wheel, able to see for great distances and talk about it. When, however, there are no building plans they are at ground level and can see only what is right in front of them. Our pastors and churches need top-of-the-wheel eyes every day.

So, my answer to the inquiring pastor above is that vision and not building is the key. I contrast two churches that I once worked with. Both had good congregations and caring pastors. Both had campaigns to construct a new facility. In one we wound up raising one million dollars more than it actually needed, and in the other we raised exactly what it sought. Both came to me after the campaign victory celebrations and asked what they should do now. Even though their results were very different, I gave them both similar answers. Start sharing a vision right now of what ministry will be like once you complete these facilities. How do you see the church changing lives and making a difference? What else do you want to do—or

IF THE PASTOR had not been regularly sharing where such gifts could go and be used wisely at the church, there is a good possibility that the donor would have given that part of his fortune to someone who had been sharing such a vision.

are you done? Has God finished with you now that the campaign is over, or does God have a new call for your church now that this particular journey is over?

In the first church, they spent way too much time celebrating that they had reached a level beyond what they asked for. They just patted each other on the back over and over and over. They formed a committee to determine what God wanted done with the extra million dollars, but after two years, they still did not have a report. Recently I heard that many of those who had made a pledge were not going to finish it out after the building was done because they had not seen what the leadership felt God wanted to do with it. Then one of them said to me, "The good news is that we got everything we needed." But did you do all that God would have you do?

The second church did not receive extra pledges, but they did get right at what their new building would cost. This pastor also formed a dream team, and three months after breaking ground on the facility, they were having town meetings and publishing what their dreams were for after completion of the new wing. At my urging, the pastor even put a dream list in the worship bulletin once a month with the cost of things needed to make those dreams come true. He had things on it from $100 to $100,000. It all added up to one million dollars. How foolish was he to think that right after having a successful capital campaign people would want to give another million dollars? Hadn't they given all they could?

> **NEVER SPEND ONE** day in ministry where you do not have a vision of where God wants you to go next and how you might get there if only you had the funds to do it.

About three months into putting out his list one of the pastor's members asked to speak to him in his office after worship was over. It was a semiactive church participant who had made a nice pledge in the just-completed campaign, but nothing extraordinary.

The man came into the office carrying the dream list sheet that had been in the bulletin that morning. He asked the pastor, "I have seen this list for the last couple of months. I assume that the church really needs these things and you believe they will make a big difference in our ministry?" The pastor acknowledged how he did feel strongly that each item on that list was needed and would be extremely helpful in allowing the church to fulfill its mission.

The man then looked up and said, "Then I want to buy

the whole thing." The puzzled look on the pastor's face showed he did not fully understand. The man went on to explain, "I just sold my business last week, and I did very well. I did not have the capital when we were in the campaign earlier this year, but I do now, and I had been wondering where would be a good place to make a gift and say thanks to God. Your list just made sense to me. Would you accept a check for the full amount or should I give it to someone else?"

The pastor told me that one of the cooler things he has experienced in his ministry was watching this man write and sign that check for one million dollars.

That one million was a capital gift. It was a one-time gift coming out of assets that were not a part of the man's regular cash flow. He had a windfall coming from the sale of his business. People usually do not schedule these windfalls. They come from an inheritance or from an unexpected rise in the stock market or just very good fortune in business. If the pastor had not been regularly sharing where such gifts could go and be used wisely at the church, there is a good possibility that the donor would have carried his desire to give part of his fortune to someone who had been sharing with him how it might be used.

There is not a college in America today that is not in a

capital campaign, in that they always have some need ready to be shared with anyone who might have a desire to give at that time. They don't tell the alumni that just because we built the science building last year we don't need a capital gift for further advancement of the school in another area. Too often the church does exactly that.

There you have it, my friend: forget your notion of capital gift always having to have a brick and mortar component. Never spend one day in ministry where you do not have a vision of where God wants you to go next and how you might get there if only you had the funds to do it. Always have an answer ready when someone walks into your office with one million dollars.

....

CHAPTER ELEVEN

Is There an Annual Campaign Program You Like?

I came to my first seminar of yours because I heard that it would show me how to do away with the annual campaign, which I just hate. At the seminar I heard you say that most cannot just eliminate the campaign right away but over time. I am not sure I understand. Can you, then, tell me what annual campaign program you like the best?

This is easily one of my most frequently asked questions. Pastors seem to really dislike the annual campaign. They treat it much like running a marathon. Everything about it seems so hard, but once it is over with there comes an

IT OFTEN LOOKS like we think there are eleven months when we have church and then one month where we have to do money.

enormous sense of relief and sometimes jubilation. They want the jubilation without the work and thus the question. Can I give them a box with all the answers in it that when opened will magically produce dollars that will mean every finance committee meeting for the next year will be a piece of cake?

My quick and easy answer is that I don't like any annual campaign program. We have gone too long relegating finances in the church to a month-long process produced out of a box. It often looks like we think there are eleven months when we have church and then one month where we have to do money. It is just a necessary evil. We have created a monster within the church, and we must remove the monster.

John Wesley said many years ago in his sermon "Use of Money" that the appropriate use of money is "largely spoken of . . . by men of the world" but that it is "not sufficiently considered by those whom God hath chosen out of the world" (paragraph 2). He was so correct.

Money and the proper or wise use of it is a topic of nearly

daily discussion in board rooms and living rooms around the world. This discussion occurs whether people have millions of dollars to spend or whether they have only a couple of dollars to spend. It is about time we started having a regular discussion about it in our sanctuary rooms. Jesus talked about what we do with our possessions more than any other topic, but today's preacher wants to limit that discussion to one sermon a year and some letters with the hope that after thirty days we won't have to talk about it anymore.

Much of the argument I wanted to make in the earlier book dealt with how we have to change this recent mindset that money is to be treated like a sex talk. It has to be done, but one does not want to do it too often, and it must be handled so delicately. On the contrary, money is so central to everything we are that it should be the most frequent of topics.

When I was in the army preparing for my first combat deployment, one of the things we trained on was putting on the chemical protective mask. We always carried it with us on our

> **MONEY IS SO** central to everything we are that it should be the most frequent of topics.

side, and we had all been to a course in basic on how to wear it, but now our leaders were saying to us that we will drill each and every day to be sure we could put it on and seal it within nine seconds. It seemed so monotonous, but I must admit that nine seconds was not much time and it was not so easy to do. The message was clear to us. If we were going to be soldiers in that unit, we would get this right and get it right every time. The reason? Our leaders wanted us to live and not die.

Money is something we all carry with us every day. It may be paper or it may be plastic, but we have it nearby all the time. Most of us can remember what our parents told us one time about saving and spending, and we all know what the preacher will say about tithing (he or she is for it). So why have regular lessons on it? We heard it already! But are we ready for all the decisions that we will have to make? Do we really understand how money could either save our lives or take them? When we get that first job and our income soars, do we know how the use of

> **OUR WHOLE LIVES** center around financial decisions, and far too often the church has just put it all in one box for one time a year.

money can save us or kill us? When that first child comes, or goes to work, or ceases to work, or the stock market gets very bullish or snores like a bear, or when we retire, do we know how to use money in ways that are pleasing to God? Our whole lives center around financial decisions, and far too often the church has just put it all in one box for one time a year.

Nothing should be taught about more regularly or practiced more diligently than how to use money wisely.

In many fundamentalist (versus mainline) churches this is how money is treated. They do not relegate it to a few weeks in the fall but talk about on an almost weekly basis how life-giving or life-destroying it can be. They discuss it plainly prior to one joining the church, and continue the discussion throughout the year. It is as much a part of who they are as that chemical mask was a part of my daily wear when in a combat environment. The mainline church needs to learn a lesson here and raise the discussion level of money in our lives prior to people joining and then continue to talk about it in their discipleship training throughout the rest of their tenure.

All of this is to say that I am not a big fan of campaigns in a box, but just wanting them to go away without substituting something else would be a huge mistake. My good friend and the coauthor of my first book, Herb Mather, wrote a delightful book called *Don't Shoot the Horse Until You've Learned to Drive the Tractor.* The point was that there is a better way to do stewardship than hold annual campaigns, but you should not toss the campaign out the window until you have developed a mature enough church to make the transition.

In the transition period, I have found it helpful to use Herb Miller's very successful program, "New Consecration Sunday." The theology is very sound and the approach is solid. It is a very good program especially in its first and second year of use. I am also a fan of doing study programs that seek to involve the entire church in studying what money means in their life. Programs like "Enough" by Adam Hamilton, "Upside Living in a Downside Economy" or "Money Matters" by Mike Slaughter, and "Fields of Gold" by Andy Stanley are all excellent in this regard.

Dr. Bob Crossman, with some assistance from me and the staff of Horizons Stewardship, has created a seven-month discipleship program called *Commitment to Christ 2020* that I am extremely excited about. It places a lot of emphasis on raising expectations and places financial stewardship as only one part of a disciple's life instead of the whole. The program is designed to start in September and end on

Easter Sunday. Each month has a different theme, and members are called each month to a new level of commitment. The monthly emphases are Commitment to Christ as Lord and Savior, Daily Prayer, Generosity, Faithful Attendance, Hands-On Service, Reading the Bible, and Witnessing to the Good News. The program is intensive and needs a number of persons to be fully effective, but it can be transformational in developing disciples and stewards.

There is also a six-week version of the same program that is a good place to start for those not quite ready to venture into seven months. It obviously is not as intensive but does follow the same themes and seeks heightened levels of commitment in six areas of discipleship.

My goal is to make financial stewardship, prayer, worship, service, evangelism, and use of the Bible tools that hang on every belt every day, ready and available to save our lives and the lives of others.

....

CHAPTER TWELVE

Can You Tell Me How to Ask for a Planned Gift?

W e don't do any planned giving at our church. I have never done it as a pastor. I heard you refer to that as clergy malpractice. Starting a program sounds like a good idea and easy enough, but you said I need to personally talk to one member a month and invite them to make a planned gift to the church. Do you have any idea how scary that is? Can you tell me how to do that?

Quick answer: yes, I know how scary that is, and I can tell you how to do that, to some extent.

The first thing you need to understand is that most

EVERY HORROR story I have heard regarding endowments came from churches that had no permanent endowment policy that controlled the funds and thus gave the donors assurance about the future use of their gifts.

everything is scary when you have never done it before. Generally only doing it makes it less scary. It was scary the first time I asked a girl out. It was scary the first time I climbed into a pulpit. It was scary the first time I flew on an airplane. It was scary the first time I went into the batter's box and had someone throw a ball at me. It was scary the first time I _____ (just fill in the blank). A lot of our fear of asking for a planned gift or any kind of gift just has to do with our not ever doing it before. It really is not something to fear. In thirty-five years of ministry, with eighteen years of doing nothing but working with Christian donors around the country, I have never had someone mind talking to me about a planned gift. You can survive this experience and, after just a couple of tries, actually get excited about it.

Before you ask someone for a planned gift for your church you have to lay the groundwork. You must have a solid endowment policy in place. This is the instrument that controls what happens to the money—both where and how it is invested and how it can be spent. It is fundamental in asking for a gift to be able to say how it will be controlled. The templates for these policies are available from most denominational foundations. They are not difficult but extremely necessary. Every horror story I have heard regarding endowments came from churches that had no permanent endowment policy that controlled the funds and thus gave the donors assurance about the future use of their gifts.

You must have a gift acceptance policy. This is a policy statement that controls exactly how a gift is accepted or rejected. You may think you would want to accept every gift offered, but you do not. You can graciously accept the pink polka-dot house slippers at Christmas and then regift them at Valentine's Day. No problem! However, if you graciously accept a piece of property that later turns out to be an environmental hazard, you have a big problem. You can't regift it. You are stuck with it and all the cost necessary to clean it up. A gift acceptance policy tells how a gift can be received. Again, templates are readily available.

Next you must be involved in some sort of systematic marketing program with the entire church. People that you

THE EASIEST THING to ask someone to do is consider remembering the church in his or her will.

talk with should have heard about the endowment program before you got to their house and hopefully have even heard of other people who are involved with it. My recommendation is that the church have a planned giving program once a quarter with a speaker along with a letter and brochure going out. A special encouragement to attend should go to those classes and individuals over the age of 65. Do not be discouraged by a small attendance initially. These events will grow each time you do them and publicize what good is coming out of them. Have testimonials from attendees and persons who have chosen to make a planned gift.

The simplest thing I would do is have a "tithe your estate" program. You start this program of encouraging everyone in the church to put a simple notation in their wills that says they want to give 10 percent to the church. It is super simple, but highly effective. Put a line on the bottom of your stationary. Have a sentence in every church bulletin or newsletter or e-mail posting. Put it on the cover of your website. "Have you remembered your church in your will?" is all you need to say. Do it every week of the year and see what your results are. It will be like a yearlong exercise program. After the year, you will not believe the results. Be sure as people commit to doing this to record their names and each week let the congregation know how many have signed up. Herd mentality will set in.

Now you are ready to start making calls. The first thing to do is make a list of those you want to see over the next six months. Take your membership roster, or senior citizens class roster, or some sheet to remind you of people and look for those you believe are your best candidates. Single older persons with no children are ideal candidates, but you won't have a lot of those. Think of people who have shown a love for the church and a desire to give in the past. Most senior citizens have children, but their children may be very successful and would not need all or any of an inheritance. Your prospects may just be very generous people who would not want to leave everything to children and are looking for a place to leave a legacy. Often you can call on a couple who just love the church, have a solid retirement picture, and would want to leave something to the church upon the first death and perhaps even more upon the second death. These are the low-hanging fruit. You can call on younger people, but you will most often not find them keen on making plans for what they believe will be something occurring in forty or fifty years.

The easiest thing to ask someone to do is consider remembering the church in his or her will. People can do this with a tithe as we discussed earlier or with a set amount. They can do it by simply putting one sentence inside their current will that one phone call to their attorneys can facilitate.

There are also numerous other vehicles that you may want to use to invite a person to consider in and around the time you are having a program about it. One is a life estate. This is where a person would gift over his or her home, stay in it until he or she dies, receive a sizeable tax deduction immediately, and then upon the person's death the home goes to the church. This is a great way for a widow to cut her tax bill and help out the church without changing her life in the present at all.

> BECOMING educated in an elementary way on these tools is not hard and will allow you to perhaps gain a huge windfall for your church later on.

Another tool is a gift annuity. An elderly person could take a CD making 2 percent interest and give that to the church as a gift in return for an annuity (annual payment). The interest on this type of charitable gift is dictated by the age of the person, but for an 80-year-old it is about 8 percent. He or she would be increasing his or her cash flow from the CD to four times as much annually until he or she dies, and then the church receives what is left of the gift principal.

There are many others, and I will not go into them now, but becoming educated in an elementary way on these tools is not hard and will allow you to perhaps gain a huge windfall for your church later on. For now, just start with the will.

What do you do once you are ready to make your first call? Have a plan. When is the best time to see this person or persons? Exactly what are you going to ask them to consider? Do you have the name of your investment advisor or foundation director or lawyer readily available if the conversation turns in such a way that the person wants to get in touch with a professional? Are there things going on in the person's life that you need to inquire about while you are there (sickness, loved ones passing, job, and so on)?

Once you are in the home and have had a chance to become comfortable with some small talk, get directly to the point. Share with them your desire to build up the church's endowment and why. Let them know what good it is doing or will do. Share any personal testimonies of donors or recipients that might be helpful. Then ask them like this: "Bill and Martha, I want to invite you to join me and others in the church to become members of our Heritage Society, which is made up of persons who have placed First Church in their wills. Would you consider a tithe or a gift from your future estate to our Eternal Flame Endowment?" Then shut up. It is very helpful to use the word "consider" whenever you make a request like this.

If they say yes, then ask them to please notify you when they have made the necessary adjustments to their wills so you can place their names in the Society and be sure they are invited to the next Society gathering, if that is all right with them. Thank them profusely, letting them know again how helpful this is to the church and will be forever. Close with a prayer.

If they say no, then thank them for all they are doing now and for letting you share about the program. Let them know you respect their decision and how much you appreciate being their pastor. Close with a prayer.

If they say they want to think about it or talk to an advisor about it, let them know that is certainly understandable. Then ask them if they have any idea when they might let you know. Don't press on this—just ask the question. Close with a prayer.

You did it. Now see, that was not so hard, was it?

CHAPTER THIRTEEN

What Do You Do in a Bad Economy?

*T*he day I finished reading your book, the stock market went down by 400 points and the news that night said that unemployment was at 10 percent. Some of my families are affected and almost all of them are afraid. Is there anything in particular I should be doing in this environment?

In 2008 the American economy started on a downward spiral that most Americans had never seen. A few of our senior citizens talked about the Great Depression and their bad memories of those tragic years. The American stock exchange major indexes saw a 50 percent retreat, and unemployment slowly crept up to 10 percent. What a fabulous opportunity!

FOR DECADES people failed to listen when preachers told them that money would not save them. They're listening now. Americans have for years been the richest people on the planet. We have thrived on a robust economy since WWII, built houses bigger than we needed, drove gas-guzzling cars without thinking about oil, bought just about anything we wanted, never thought much of saving but loved credit, and in general supported ourselves and people all over the world with our spending. We truly believed that bigger barns would save us and that good times would just roll and roll and roll. In so many ways, that came to a halt as the economy imploded in late 2008 and 2009. People who had figured their 401k would keep gaining 10-20 percent a year now saw those portfolios cut in half. People who purchased houses they could not afford on the belief that they could sell it at a great profit in just a year or two now saw that house worth far less than they paid for it and a mortgage company that needed payment. Some of America's great companies like Bear Stearns, AIG, Lehman Brothers, General Motors, and Merrill Lynch either folded or had to be bailed out by a government loan. What a great opportunity!

The opportunity available was that the American church could now proclaim a gospel that was never-changing and a Lord that was everlasting and get heard. For decades preachers could not get an audience when they wanted to preach that money would not save people; there was so much money few paid close attention. "Yes, I heard the preacher on Sunday," they would say, "but I also got a call from my broker on Monday who said I had just made a bundle." Others would chime in, "I am not satisfied. I feel frustrated. I don't feel complete. I am depressed. I think I will take my credit card and go shop."

Our pews were full of people who could not see the answer that was on the altar of their churches for the bank statements that were in their mailboxes. They truly believed that more stuff and an even bigger bank account would solve their

WE CAN NOW talk about how temporary all this is and how eternal life is offered through Jesus Christ. We can talk about the need to nourish our souls more than our portfolio. We can talk about how all the money in the world will not prevent cancers or heartaches or death.

problems. Meanwhile, teenage pregnancies rose precipitously, divorce rates continued to go up, greed was ruling Wall Street and companies like Enron, wars were being waged just to keep the oil flowing and the price down, and Americans just said, " If two cars don't make me happy, I will try three. If that five-day cruise did not do it, I will try a 10-day cruise. If my family boat didn't work, I will try a cabin cruiser. If the new home doesn't make us happy, then I will add a lake house." Meanwhile the preachers just started preaching "God loves you and expects very little" sermons. Now we have an opportunity.

What is the opportunity in the midst of the crisis? The opportunity is that people who for decades would not listen to us are now ready and in many instances begging us to speak. To people wondering if there is an answer, we can say yes and tell them about a life greater than this one. We can talk about how temporary all this is and how eternal life is offered through Jesus Christ. We can talk about how it is one's soul that needs to be nourished more

> **PEOPLE IN THE**
> American church could easily proclaim how much they loved Jesus when their bank accounts were overflowing.

than one's portfolio. We can talk about how all the money in the world will not prevent cancers or heartaches or death, but we have a word for the Good Friday moments, and it is Easter. This is a time to raise up what faith is all about after

NOW IS A time for us to say that today is but a grain of sand when compared with eternity. Now is the time for us to call people to grounding not based on sand but rock. Now is the time.

going years with parishioners with shut ears. We have a real opportunity to get people to hear, but we have to speak.

A crisis can help define us like nothing else. It is easy to talk about something you do not feel you will ever have to do. I spent 18 years in the Army Reserve and remember prior to 1991 how easy it was for soldiers I trained with to say they would go when called. Then one day the President called and said he needed them in Saudi Arabia. Many found out that their commitment to the Army was not quite as strong as they thought it was and wanted out. It is easy to say that you would be strong in the face of a cancer invading your body until one day you have that cancer.

People in the American church could easily proclaim how much they loved Jesus when their bank accounts were overflowing. They could say that they had faith in Christ above all else, but when suddenly they did not have the retirement accounts they felt they needed, were they able to rely on faith or did fear overwhelm? This is our moment and this is our time to raise up an answer and be heard.

Here are some things I have been sharing with many who have called:

Don't Panic

You, the preacher, must have confidence in our sovereign God to lead you and the church through this. It has astounded me that I have gotten so many inquiries from so many preachers who seemed just scared to death about what would happen to their churches with an economy that was in crisis. Far too many acted just like Aaron when things got a bit tough in the wilderness. They ceased to look at their God and instead put trust in a golden calf. They have cried out as leaders did against Joshua and Caleb saying, "Sure I know what God says, but did you see the news last night (giants on the other side)?" Fear quickly overcame faith as the dominant controller of one church after another. Do we not believe that the Via Dolarosa is mightier than Wall Street? Now is a time for us to be bold not shy.

> NOW IS THE time to be sharing with them what role money should have in their lives and how wealth is not their God, refuge, or strength.

Now is a time for us to remind people of how firm a foundation we believe in. Now is a time for us to say that today is but a grain of sand when compared with eternity. Now is the time for us to call people to grounding not based on sand but rock. Now is the time.

Of course, the first step is for the preacher to do some soul-searching. Is your hope grounded on faith or is it more on your own 403b? How much do you read your Bible compared to listening to CNBC? Are you truly convinced that Jesus is the answer, or do you put a bit more stock in your net worth statement? Where is "stuff" in your own life? The crisis can do a lot for the preacher as well as the church member. We too have become careless with things and needed to be slapped a bit to help us see the parting sea versus the on-rushing army.

Tell More Stories

When times are hard, go back to the basics and to the fundamentals. Redouble your efforts to tell your churches stories of how you are changing lives and making a difference. People still have and will give money, but they will be much more discriminating. Instead of giving to 10 charities when times were easier, they will give to one or two. You want to be sure your stories are known so that people will choose you.

Be a Servant Church

Far too many churches have responded to the economic crisis by crying, "Oh, woe is me." They have just asked for more and more. You need to communicate clearly that you know some of your people are in fiscal distress and that the church wants to assist. Encourage them to contact a pastor. Prepare a team to help families in need. Make it clear that the church remains focused on giving, not receiving. Your best chance to receive is for you to give.

Be Honest

Be upfront about the condition of the church in the crisis without crying that the ship is sinking. Let them know what stresses you may be under and how those who are able might help. Do this in e-mails or letters and not from the pulpit.

A CHURCH THAT does not learn from hard times is a dumb church.

Preach, Preach, Preach

Now is the time to be sharing with them what role money should have in their lives and how wealth is not their God, refuge, or strength. As I said earlier, people are more open now than ever before to hearing sermons on money. There is no better time to talk about it than during an economic crisis. I have heard several preachers tell me they have done a 4- or 5-part series on money, advertized it throughout the community, and had huge crowds of visitors. People are looking for answers. Don't disappoint!

Visit Your Major Donors

A few weeks ago I had something happen that has never happened before. I got a call from both American Airlines and from Avis Rental Car. Both were inquiring about my plans to use them in my business in the upcoming year.

They said they were calling their most frequent customers to assess the upcoming business climate. It was a smart thing for them to do. The economic downturn will have an effect on their companies but just how much is probably best determined by actually talking to their best customers.

Your church probably has about 5-10 percent of your donors supporting 70-80 percent of your budget. Talk to them. Ask them how they are doing and what their plans are in the midst of what is occurring in the country. If most all of them are good to go then you probably will not experience any serious issues. If several of them have had setbacks and will significantly decrease their giving, then you have a problem to work on.

The bottom line is don't guess. Go ask! If it was smart for American Airlines and Avis to ask, then why not you?

Start a Weekly Prayer Group

Right after 9-11 I heard of many churches that were having special prayer gatherings. In the midst of the uncertainty and fear, members of the congregation were assembling for prayer. Since the economy did not tank at one set moment, I did not hear of nearly as many doing the same thing during this crisis. People and churches fell into a trap of believing that the cures were to be found by bankers and legislators and that the church had little to offer. I believe the cure for our economic woes lies in our spiritual condition far more than our economic condition. A weekly prayer gathering of all church leaders where you pray for the nation, world, economy, and church will help center people on God's voice in this effort and turn our hearts on seeking spiritual solutions rather than just financial ones. It may not last more than 5 minutes, but it will be a powerful 5 minutes.

Do Planned Giving Now

Churches that have strong endowments are weathering the storm much better than those that do not. The interest from these nonrestricted funds can fill in the gaps when unforeseen events occur. If you don't have a planned giving program in place it will not help you through these times, but you could plant a seed that will help the church and a future pastor, while at the same time hoping that some other pastor is thinking of you by planting the seed where he or she is.

Start Financial Planning Classes Yesterday

Programs like Financial Peace University, Crown, and others are excellent to assist your congregation in avoiding the kinds of debt decisions that got them in trouble. They teach people how to manage their finances like Christians who put God first in their lives. People are clamoring for classes such as this, and any church that offers them frequently is doing its community a great service.

My hope is that as you are reading this the economy is strong, fear has subsided, and people are optimistic. A church that does not learn from hard times, however, is a dumb church. Do not let your people forget those days, and begin now to lay a solid faith foundation under their lives so that the next time the storms come, those storms will not destroy the house. You should look at the economic crash like a heart attack you lived through. You dodged a bullet, and now you must make changes (lifestyle, diet, exercise, and so on) to prevent another one. You cannot get rid of all the fatty foods in the world, but you can change how often you eat them. You cannot change the way the whole world does business, but you can affect how your congregation reacts to the consequences of that business.

....

CHAPTER FOURTEEN

Will You Talk to My Spouse?

*C*lif, *I am embarrassed about my giving. I have been a*
pastor for fifteen years and I do believe in tithing, but I
have never practiced it. My wife just does not see things
the same as I do. She supports me in most everything I want to do
as a preacher, but when it comes to giving she thinks that is way
too much. I don't know what to do. I feel like I need to support my
church, but I have to respect my wife, too. Would you come over
and talk to her for me?

I was not shy in *Not Your Parents' Offering Plate* in calling
for pastors to be leaders in financial stewardship with their
churches. One of my pet phrases has been, "The sheep

I WANT TO encourage any pastor struggling with this issue to talk to a marriage counselor.

won't go where the shepherd won't lead." If our pastors cannot set examples in ministry, including giving, then we just cannot expect our members to practice it. Not only must we practice, but I offered that we must be willing on a regular basis to witness to it.

The pastor who asked the question above did it privately as he and I stood on his parking lot following a meeting with his finance committee. He knew that I was aware of his giving, but I had not had the opportunity to bring it up with him. His church was in financial difficulty, and I had been called in to study the issues and offer solutions. He knew that he was one of the problems. He also felt genuinely stuck and was very frustrated. I hurt for him.

The first word out of my mouth was, "No." He was a bit taken aback. I then told him that it just was not my place to get into his married life and this probably had more to do with his marriage than with his giving. I suspected that there were other things he and his wife struggled with regarding the practices of the faith. To him his ministry was a calling. To her it was a way they paid the bills. They were a long way apart.

One thing I did wonder about was whether his wife saw his giving as a business decision or as a religious/faith conviction. My guess was that she saw it as a business decision that she had every right to influence, just like a decision on whether to buy a new car or not. Had he ever sat down and had a discussion with her about how it was faith that was driving this conviction? He, of course, needed to answer that question first.

Since this pastor first approached me with this request, I have talked with a number of pastors who have the same struggles in their homes. The pastor and spouse are just on different planets when it comes to finances. He may want to save, and she wants to spend. She may want to give, and he wants to keep. He may want some new tools, and she wants a new living room set. The issue is probably not just finances related to church, but finances overall in the marriage.

I am not a marriage counselor, and this is not a marriage book. I want to encourage any pastor struggling with this issue to talk to a marriage counselor. For a pastor, giving to the church should be as fundamental as preaching. It is what we do, and it is who we are. I also recognize that our spouses are usually not clergy or even sometimes Christian, so it may not be fundamental for them. Marriage is a partnership where two persons come together to help the goals of the other come true. It is the partnership that I am concerned with here and not whether this pastor tithes or not. I hope he or she will work with a professional, not so he or she starts giving, but so the partnership of the marriage can be understood and strengthened for the good of the family. In other words, this issue is much larger than tithing, and one needs to take it seriously as a symptom of a greater illness.

....

CHAPTER FIFTEEN

Aren't Sex and Money Taboo in Public?

I was raised believing that you did not talk about sex or money in public. I have tended to stick to that as a pastor, and my people seem to appreciate it. Only when I am in deer camp with a bunch of guys do I hear anyone talk about sex and it is never serious. Even there I don't hear anyone talk about money. Are you saying that we need to be talking about money more in church and even individual's money as far as their giving goes?

Yes, I am, but I would not want the discussion held in church to be equated with what I have also heard at a hunting camp. We need to talk about both sex and money a

BOTH SEX AND money should be at the forefront of our preaching because they are at the root of much of society's problems.

lot more in the church, but not in the same vein as you reference.

Your question gets right at the heart of much of the problem we have in the church about both sex and money. They have become taboo subjects in our pulpits, classrooms, study groups, and other arenas of spiritual growth. We have wrongly acted like neither has anything to do with spirituality or our relationship with God. In fact, both should be at the forefront of our preaching because they are at the root of much of society's problems. It gets back to what our motives are for having the discussion. Certainly in some forums both sex and money would be very inappropriate issues to discuss, but in others they would be extremely appropriate, and in fact to not discuss them might be clergy malpractice.

I went to see my doctor last week. While there he asked me to take off my clothes. Now taking off one's clothes is a pretty private matter, but I did not question his right to ask for that. He needed to examine me from head to toe to do his job properly. In fact, if he had tried to do the exam that

I needed most and did not ask me to disrobe he would not be practicing good medicine. I did as he asked and trusted him to handle his exam in the appropriate manner. During that same exam he wanted to ask me some questions about my lifestyle. It was easy to answer him on exercise and diet, but then he probed into my sexual habits and desires, and I admit I got a bit uncomfortable. He asked me about how much I was working and how I was handling anxiety and stress. That makes me uncomfortable as well. I talked to him honestly about all of that, and when my time was done he told me what he felt I needed to do to be as physically healthy as possible. I trust that all of my conversations with him will be confidential within his office. I know that his nurse will need to have some of the information, as will the person at billing, and a lab technician. However, I believe that the general public will not know what I have shared, and I am

> IF MY DOCTOR and my banker had not asked questions about these uncomfortable matters, they wouldn't have been doing their jobs. How, then, is it different for pastors to ask questions about money?

good with that. He did his job, and I am better off because of it.

Later that day I went to see my banker about some of my business plans. For us to do what we need to do we will need some money up front, and I was seeking his partnership with a loan. He wanted to know a lot of things about my financial welfare. His job was to help me while, at the same time, looking out for the well-being of the bank that employed him. If he makes a bad business decision and gives me money that I cannot afford to pay back then he hurts me, himself, his employer, and perhaps someone else who might have used the money more wisely. He needs information to do his job properly.

I talked to him about how much I made last year. I gave him a copy of my last two tax returns. I took him a copy of a profit/loss statement on my business, and he put all of them in a file to study. He also talked to me about how much I thought I would earn this year and in future years. He wanted to know some specifics about my business strategy and how we intended to compete with other companies. It was a conversation that I do not have with very many people, and some parts of it were a bit uncomfortable, but I knew he needed to ask and I needed to share the answers as best as I could. When we were done we shook hands, and he

said he would call me
in a couple of days. I
knew that his secre-
tary was going to
write up what we had
talked about and he
would be having a

> ## WHY WOULD
> we want to pretend that
> our financial lives are not
> a reflection of our
> spiritual lives?

conversation with the president of the bank about my request. It was also highly likely that all of this information would then be shared with the bank's loan committee or even board before I got my answer. I trusted that our conversation and the information he was in possession of would remain within the bank, and I never even considered that I might walk into the barber shop and find out it had been made public. A bank that let out confidential information would not remain a viable bank for long.

Later that evening as a member of the church's board, I dropped in on the pastor to offer my opinion on a decision the church was making. As we talked he changed the subject to ask me some questions regarding my lack of giving to the church. He noted that my family gave only about $1,000 to the general fund of the church and failed to make a pledge to the building fund. He asked if we were all right and was there anything he should know or do. He was concerned that the level of giving reflected issues within my soul and spirit and, as my pastor, wanted to inquire on how he might help. I was angry. How dare he look into my giving and ask me about my financial matters. This was an issue between me and God, and I did not want him poking his nose into my business.

Do you see the irony of my day? It did not bother me to share the most intimate details about my private life with my physician because I wanted him to do his job well. If he does his job well then I am in better physical health and I might live longer.

It did not bother me to share very intimate details about my financial affairs with my banker because I wanted him to do his job well. If he does his job well then I am in better financial condition and my business might prosper.

What does it profit me, however, to gain the whole world if I lose my soul? My pastor is the one who is there to advise me on how to care for my soul. He is there to help see that I have not only physical life and financial life but also everlasting life. In fact, the part of me that he is to help me with will have a profound effect on both my physical and financial well-being. If my pastor does not ask me such questions, he is not looking out for what is best for me. He is not doing his job to the fullest extent. He is like a physician who saw a bad lab result and did not report to me a remedy. He is like a banker who saw pending bankruptcy and did not let me know how to avoid it. They would both be extremely negligent and perhaps lose their licenses or jobs over it.

WE CAN'T HAVE two masters, money and God. It is one or the other. The job of every pastor is to help God come out on top and to do that he or she must work faithfully and tirelessly to remove money from that position.

Why is it that our pastors are not encouraged more to do their jobs? Why is it that we do not treat sin as a disease that our pastors may know the cure for? Why would we want to pretend that our financial lives are not a reflection of our spiritual lives? Do we not care about our soul's condition? If a pastor sees that someone in leadership in the church is not giving and supporting the church, is the pastor not hurting the person and the church (his or her business) by keeping such a secret? Could it be considered clergy malpractice to see the above person's giving record and not report it appropriately out of concern for the person first and the church second?

The reason we do not report such giving behavior even when clearly seen by a pastor is simply that giving is so endemic to the sin of so many. The vast majority of the people in our churches and even those in leadership love money more than they do God, and they do not want the preacher reminding them too often of their sin. Even when we note this sin in others it is not easily accepted by the rest as a pastor doing his or her job because we fear we will be next. Therefore, we take on a position of silence and allow the sinners to run the church. It takes guts to be a prophet, yet that is what ministers are called to be.

I do not advocate that we start next Sunday by mounting our soapboxes and proclaiming that the rules about money and the church are going to change starting right now. Such a move as that would blow up before any good could come from it. It is time, however, that we begin this dialog and remove money from the sacrosanct arena. We must help our people see the ruin that the use and love of money is causing in their lives. If we are going to truly become spiritually healthy, we must begin to break down this barrier that says we will not talk about it from the pulpit or in the living room. It should begin in public forums, starting with a plainly shared series of sermons on money. Then it must move to small groups, and eventually it must get to where the congregation respects the minister who will make honest inquiry into one's spiritual well-being upon reflection of what he or she is giving. We can't have two masters, money and God. It is one or the other. The job of every pastor is to help God come out on top and to do that he or she must work faithfully and tirelessly to remove money from that position.

I have rejoiced recently in seeing that more and more of our churches are venturing out to discuss AIDS, abortion, homosexuality, teenage pregnancy, STDs, abstinence, and other such issues all related to our sexual lives. These issues have spiritual consequences and spiritual answers. Much of it has to do with what we do in our bedrooms, but God lives in bedrooms, too. The church must not be silent for the sake of the souls it is responsible for. Maybe money will be next.

....

CHAPTER SIXTEEN

How Do I Get the Right Leaders in the Right Places?

*I*f I am going to have any success implementing these changes you call for in our attitude and culture regarding giving in the church, I am going to have to have a real overhaul of my leadership people. How do I get the people in place to help me implement much of this?

This is a great question, and it reflects a pastor who knows the reality of change. If he or she does not have the right people in the right places, he or she can preach all day long and will see very little result from the labor. To make significant change will require leadership to boldly get behind the changes.

A PASTOR SEEKING to bring about a radical change in the way a church understands financial stewardship must have very strong stewards in positions of leadership.

Someone asked me the other day who I thought would win in a football game if one team was coached by Bear Bryant and the other was coached by Knute Rockne. I pondered it for just a second, and then he grinned and said, "The one with the best players." He was so right. A coach can only do so much and then it is up to the players to win the game. In that same vein, I was reading about a school that had hired a new coach after going through a dismal season. One interviewer asked the athletic director what he wanted the new coach to do first, and he quickly fired back, "Recruit better players."

If a pastor has any hope in turning a church around or in creating a great church, that hope will begin with the right lay leaders in place. It does not have to happen immediately, but it is important for a pastor seeking to bring about a radical change in the way a church understands financial stewardship to have very strong stewards in positions of leadership to work with him or her through what will potentially be a long process.

Not too long ago a pastor asked me to come and do a thorough review of what his church was doing in financial stewardship. They weren't meeting their budget, which was already minimal, and no new ministries had gotten started in about two years. The pastor said to me, "We are just broken when it comes to our finances, and we look forward to your counsel."

One of the areas that stood out to me after reviewing considerable data from the church was the makeup of the finance committee. In this rather large suburban church this group consisted of fourteen people, twelve of whom were men over 55 who were mostly involved in financial occupations. On it were bankers, financial advisors, CPAs, CFOs, and insurance professionals. There were a couple of retired persons, but for the most part the group was employed in mostly significant positions. Six of them even owned their own businesses. It was obvious from the

> **FAR TOO OFTEN,** churches place people in positions of financial authority because they know something about money. The problem is that they do not know anything about Jesus.

makeup that this was a power group that undoubtedly wielded great influence on the church.

I took their names and compared it to a list I had of the top 75 donors in the church. These were people who all gave at least $3,000 a year to this church. To my shock, only four of the fourteen were on that list, and the chairperson was not one of those four. I can remember thinking that I should probably just fold the entire study right there, return the downpayment, and go on to something else. Nothing was going to happen with my recommendations. Well, I ignored that little voice and prepared my report on how this church needed to make adjustments and changes in its stewardship culture to move ahead. On the night I presented it, you could have heard a pin drop in the room. There were few questions. I left them and returned home. Two weeks later the pastor called to thank me and give me an update. "I wanted you to know," he said, "the finance committee has tabled moving forward with your report until an unnamed date in the future. I doubt it will ever see the light of day." He apologized, but there was no need. I felt for him. His ministry was going to be negatively affected by these "players," and until he gets some new recruits he will have a hard time moving in a positive direction to be the church he knows it is being called to be.

Far too often, I see pastors and church nominations groups place people into positions where they have great say-so over how God's money is used just

> **IT IS FAR MORE** important for individual families to learn how to give generously than for God (or the church) to receive.

because these people know something about money. The problem is that they do not know anything about Jesus. We must remember what business we are in. We are in the disciple-making business. We are in the soul-saving business. We are in the life-changing business. We are not in the money business. Money has one purpose in the church and that is to make disciples. Its purpose is not to accrue in a reserve fund just so someone can proclaim that the budget is balanced one day.

These people with influence over money in the church must also know that extravagant generosity is what is sought and not just a certain amount of money. It is far more important for individual families to learn how to give generously than for God (or the church) to receive. Giving is one of the ways that we nourish our souls to stay in proper alignment with our Lord. If you have a committee made up of persons who do not understand or refuse to accept this basic fundamental truth about our faith, then you have got the wrong players in the wrong positions. You have placed infants in positions that requires mature Christians. To move forward you have to get the right players in place.

Doing this begins with your board or leadership body defining exactly what your mission is. Everything must flow from there. To achieve this mission you will need resources. The most important resource is people. What are those positions? How many staff, and how many lay volunteers? What are the criteria for those who serve? Exactly what is expected of those who commit to serve? Even if your denomination has a rule book, you should write your own around your mission.

It would be assumed that all those serving from the pastor on down would be required to exhibit cer-

> ANYONE WHO wants to lead in the church should be committed to tithing as a minimum level of giving. I don't see any other standard given in Scripture that we are to measure our giving by than the tithe.

tain leadership qualities. This makes sense in any organization whether it is business, or church, or government. Everyone on your ruling body should understand this premise. Now what are those leadership qualities for YOUR CHURCH? Remember, just because someone shows that they can lead somewhere does not mean that they can lead anywhere. I may be a great general, but I would not be a good football coach. I may be a great corporate executive but not a great leader in the body of Christ. Again, remember who YOU are.

It seems to me that anyone who wants to lead in the church should, at a minimum, be a part of your worship experience at least 75 percent of the year. Worship is perhaps the most important thing you do, and they must be intimately related to it to help guide it.

Anyone who wants to lead in the church should at a minimum be a part of a study group where they are growing in the faith. It can be Sunday school, small group study, or a weekly Bible class. Nurturing people is a key part of what the church does, and a leader must understand it and be a part of it to help guide that part of the church.

Anyone who wants to lead in the church should, at a minimum, be involved in serving others outside the church. The church is called to give itself away to those not in the church. It is in giving of ourselves that people come to know the meaning of the cross. Anyone who is to lead must be in at least one mission experience each year.

Anyone who wants to lead in the church should be committed to tithing as a minimum level of giving. I don't see any other standard given in Scripture by which we are to measure our giving than the tithe. Some were called to give much more, but I see none who were asked to give less. Remember you are selecting leaders here and not making a requirement for people who are seekers or who want to come to the church. These are those who will lead.

One or more of the above criteria demonstrate that someone loves Jesus Christ as their Lord and Savior with all his or her heart and soul and mind and strength. If he or she did not do the above, and were physically able, I would have to wonder what else was influencing his or her heart.

Ask your leaders this when you bring this matter to the table. Would they want a pastor who did not want to be in worship three-fourths of the time? Would they want a pastor who did not study the Bible regularly? Would they want a pastor who did not want to serve others? Would they want a pastor who did not give generously?

My guess is they will say no, and the reason is they want a pastor to lead. Exactly! We don't just need our pastors to lead; we also need our laity to lead. If a person accepts a position of leadership then he or she needs to know the responsibilities that go with that leadership. Every great church that I know of has leaders in place from pastor to staff to lay volunteers who meet or exceed the above-mentioned criteria.

The first step then is to establish the criteria. Then once it is in place, it should be made public so people will know what their leaders have committed to do and be. Then a process needs to be established where those who are being asked to serve can commit to maintaining the standard for leaders. At a minimum, a covenant should be prepared that each would sign. The pastor should be the first to sign and then paid staff. If some sort of nomination process takes place where a committee must select persons who are then voted on, the pastor should be asked to ascertain for the committee ahead of time, to the best of his or her ability, whether there will be a problem with any individual meeting the standard so as not to embarrass anyone.

This will take some doing, but it must be done for you to have any hope of radically changing the culture of stewardship and discipleship. Take it slow and begin with mission understanding. Go from there to a church policy on leadership, and then from there to recruiting new and better players. Hopefully it will lead you to a lot more victories as a church.

CHAPTER SEVENTEEN

Can You Just Make It Simple for Me?

C *lif, this is the third seminar I have attended. The first time I came because I had nothing else to do that day. The second time I wanted to come and bring some of my parishioners. This time I am here because it still feels a bit overwhelming. Can you just make it real simple for me on just how to get started?*

I am very sympathetic toward this young pastor. I can remember being exactly where he is. I remember going to hear some guy speak on how he had all the answers and leaving either bored to death or feeling overwhelmed with how to get started on creating my own solutions. Quite often in the maze of trying to figure it out while I still had a complicated church to run, I would just give up and go back to what I had been doing. Change, especially a cultural change, is so very hard.

I also want this pastor to know of my own confession. When I was in his shoes, I did not do everything right either. A part of what I am sharing is what I have learned after no longer having to preach a sermon every seven days, officiate burials on a moment's notice, and counsel the bereaved, which might include a spouse, sibling, child, parent, or friend. Then I would have to attend three evening meetings a week dealing with everything from a women's bazaar to a men's BBQ, hiring a children's director, or buying cribs for the nursery. In between this I would field calls and e-mails from people who loved last week's sermon, hated last week's sermon, wanted to find Jesus by midnight, did not think they knew Jesus anymore, drank too much last Saturday, wanted to divorce the one who drank too much last Saturday, failed at school, graduated from school, and wondered when I was going to come cut the grass. Being a pastor is one of the hardest jobs in the world, and I have enormous empathy for all who serve.

I have learned much of what I have written in this book and in the previous two books because I have had time to talk with donors and understand how they think and what makes them act in the ways they do. I have had time to serve nearly 400 local churches, both large and small, in one fashion or another because I did not have the burden of being a pastor of a local church. I can certainly appreciate someone wanting the simple rules version of how to make a difference and bring about some progress without the burden of a multi-year plan. So what follows is the Clif's notes for stewardship change:

Simple Rules to Follow Now

TITHE

This involves no one but yourself and your spouse, if you have one. It is a spiritual decision that you can make in your own home without involving anyone else. You need to begin to tithe by giving 10 percent of what you would be making if you had a real-world salary: 10

> **THANK PEOPLE**
> for faithfully teaching a class, taking kids on a mission trip, mowing the church lawn, and, of course, giving generously.

percent of your gross salary, including rental value of the parsonage or housing allowance, and the value of any other perks that come your way. Then go witness to it. When you do that witness be as plain as you can. Spell out the numbers to your people. If you just made the decision, then confess to them that you were not there before, but you are now and how and why you made the decision. This is leadership, and it is RULE NUMBER ONE! If you cannot do this, then do not go on to Rule Two.

WRITE TEN THANK YOU NOTES A WEEK

Again this is something you can do without involving anyone else. You can start tomorrow. The key here is to thank people who genuinely deserve it. For instance, one pastor asked me if he should thank every single donor. No, you should reserve a thank you note for those who have exemplified behavior

> ALL EXEMPLARY giving begins with people knowing your mission and wanting to be a part of it. Yet I find most church members cannot define for me what the mission of their church is.

that is of the sort that you want to reinforce. Thank people for faithfully teaching a class, taking kids on a mission trip, mowing the church lawn, and, of course, giving generously.

START USING TESTIMONIES IN WORSHIP

Worship is almost always the prerogative of the pastor. I cannot imagine many who would object if you chose for one or two minutes right before the offering to have someone share how Christ or the church has changed or affected his or her life. You don't need a budget for this. You don't really need permission for this. You don't have to involve others in this, except, of course, to speak. You won't want to keep full responsibility for this for long because of the time required to find the testifier and prep them, but you can get it started, and once people see it you can hand it off.

GET MISSION FOCUSED

You can set up a task force to start focusing on what the real mission of the church is or should be. Get people united around a common purpose. All exemplary giving begins with people knowing your mission and wanting to be a part of it. Yet I find most church members cannot define for me what the mission of their church is. They really aren't sure what they are supporting, have obviously little passion for the unknown, and wind up just giving because it seemed like the right thing to do. This task force will not require much money, if any, and it can be established with just the pastor asking for a group to assist him or her in defining what the mission of the church should be. Once they arrive at a good conclusion you can get it approved through official channels. A word of caution—don't just let them get by with something like "make disciples." Push them to define exactly what they understand that to be as stated by Jesus and understood by the twenty-first-century church.

VISION PREACHING

Once you and your mission task force have defined your mission, you should spend time in prayer and study on exactly what you feel God wants you to be doing to fulfill that mission. That is vision. This sense of God's call should become a sermon series where you seek to help your people understand where God has encouraged you to lead them. More than any time in my ministry I am hearing church laity tell me they want to be led. They are bewildered by a world at war and a shaky economy. They want their pastor to give them guidance on where they should go. Give it to them as God has given it to you. This is what generates great generosity and is how God will eventually change the world. This, too, you can do without having to ask permission or raise the budget.

I am tempted to go on with several more things you could do now, but why don't you start here? And when you get all these done, go back and read *Not Your Parents' Offering Plate* again. You will get lots of other ideas on what should come next.

CPSIA information can be obtained at www.ICGtesting.com
Printed in the USA
LVOW06s1222160414

381857LV00002B/2/P